나혼자 끝내는
독학 한국어
첫걸음

나혼자 끝내는 독학 한국어 첫걸음
Super Easy Korean for Beginners: A Self-Study Book

지은이 이혜현
펴낸이 임상진
펴낸곳 (주)넥서스

초판 1쇄 발행 2020년 3월 17일
초판 3쇄 발행 2023년 8월 30일

출판신고 1992년 4월 3일 제311-2002-2호
10880 경기도 파주시 지목로 5
Tel (02)330-5500 Fax (02)330-5555

ISBN 979-11-6165-907-7 13710

www.nexusbook.com

나 혼자 끝내는
독학 한국어
첫걸음

Lee Hyehyun

Super Easy Korean
for Beginners:
A Self-Study Book

넥서스

For Learners
Studying Korean Basics

This book is designed to help people who begin to study Korean at the basic level. Learners will be able to practice speaking, memorize words and understand grammar through dialog and review tests. The lessons in this book have been carefully chosen to help the learners understand a range of topics for everyday talk. There are also culture sections to learn about Korean life, customs and traditions. For further study and practice, 8 learning materials including a vocabulary note, MP3 files, workbook, etc. are also available.

Along with adorable illustrations and useful expressions, get started to study Korean with ease. By the end of the course, you will finally understand how the language really works. Just feel confident and let's go ahead! Good luck!

How To Learn 'Super Easy Korean'

1 Watch video lectures. You can learn Korean with ease through the author's video lectures.

2 This is where you can learn the grammar and phrases. Memorize the words with audio recordings. There are simple tests that you can check what you've learned.

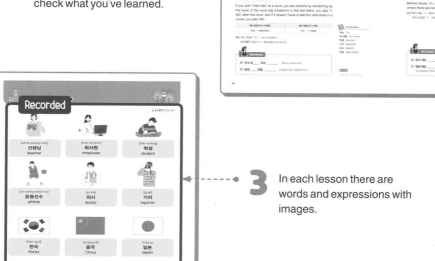

3 In each lesson there are words and expressions with images.

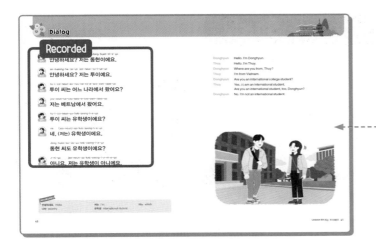

4 You can practice speaking with useful dialog. There is an audio for you to learn how to pronounce all the sentences.

6 You can look around some interesting Korean cultures.

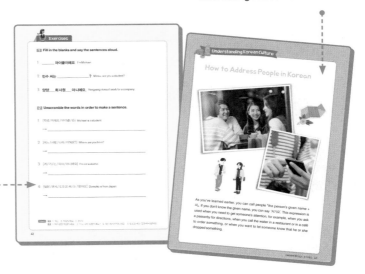

5 Test yourself on the grammar and vocabulary and check how much you can remember.

7 You can review the sentences from the book while you watch videos.

8 Memorizing words is the basic step of learning a language. It could be easier for you to study when you watch a video.

8 Learning Materials for Self-Study

Video Lectures

You can learn Korean with ease through the author's video lectures.

Videos for Reviewing

You can review the sentences from the book while you watch videos.

Videos for Words

You can review the words from the book while you watch videos.

MP3 for Listening

You can listen to the pronunciation of each sentence and word by Korean native speakers.

MP3 for Speaking

You can repeat after Korean native speakers and practice shadowing.

Word Lists

With portable word lists, you can review the words in the book.

Picture Words

The words with pictures help you memorize the words more effectively.

Workbook

You can practice Korean with the workbook by writing words, sentences.

Online

How to use 8 learning materials

1

Scan QR codes in the book.

2

Visit nexusbook.com and download free video lectures.

넥서스북

Super Easy Korean for Beginners

베스트셀러
새로나온책
시리즈
분야별책

❶ Visit our website.
www.nexusbook.com
❷ Click the download button.

책 소개	MP3 / 부가자료	목차

MP3 무료 | 1 개 | 40.64 MB

- MP3파일 다운로드는 회원 전용 서비스이며, 유료상품이 포함되어 있습니다.
  로그인 후 이용해 주세요.
- 다운로드는 PC에서만 제공하며, 스마트폰에서는 다운로드 할 수 없습니다.
- MP3파일은 압축되어 1개(용량이 큰 경우에는 2개 이상)의 ZIP 파일로 제공됩니다.
  받으신 파일은 압축을 풀고 사용하시기 바랍니다.

3

Search for 〈Super Easy Korean for Beginners: A Self-Study Book〉 on Youtube.

Study Planner

	Video Lectures	Book Listen with MP3 and check how many times you have studied.	Videos for Reviewing	Word Lists	Videos for Words
Lesson 01	📺	① ② ③ 16~25p			
Lesson 02	📺	① ② ③ 26~33p			
Lesson 03	📺	① ② ③ 34~43p	📹	📝 2p	📝
Lesson 04	📺	① ② ③ 44~53p	📹	📝 3p	📝
Lesson 05	📺	① ② ③ 54~63p	📹	📝 4p	📝
Lesson 06	📺	① ② ③ 64~73p	📹	📝 5~6p	📝
Lesson 07	📺	① ② ③ 74~83p	📹	📝 7p	📝
Lesson 08		① ② ③ 84~89p			
Lesson 09	📺	① ② ③ 90~99p	📹	📝 8p	📝

	Video Lectures	Book Listen with MP3 and check how many times you have studied.			Videos for Reviewing	Word Lists	Videos for Words
Lesson 10	▶	1	2	3 100~109p	▶	9p	✎
Lesson 11	▶	1	2	3 110~119p	▶	10p	✎
Lesson 12	▶	1	2	3 120~129p	▶	11p	✎
Lesson 13	▶	1	2	3 130~139p	▶	12~13p	✎
Lesson 14	▶	1	2	3 140~149p	▶	14p	✎
Lesson 15	▶	1	2	3 150~159p	▶	15p	✎
Lesson 16	▶	1	2	3 160~169p	▶	16~17p	✎
Lesson 17		1	2	3 170~175p			

Contents

Lesson 01

한글 Hangul   16

- ☐ Vowels (1)
- ☐ Combination of consonants and vowels (1)
- ☐ Consonants (2)
- ☐ Batchim (2)
- ☐ Combination of consonants and vowels (2)
- ☐ Consonants (1)
- ☐ Vowels (2)
- ☐ Batchim (1)
- ☐ Lenition

Lesson 02

인사 표현 Greetings   26

- ☐ When meeting someone
- ☐ Apologizing
- ☐ Congratulating
- ☐ When coming home
- ☐ When asking about health, etc.
- ☐ When going to bed
- ☐ New Year Greetings
- ☐ When leaving someone
- ☐ Thanking
- ☐ When going out
- ☐ When visiting someone
- ☐ Before/after meals
- ☐ When asking a question to stranger

Lesson 03

저는 투이예요. I'm Thuy.   34

- ☐ noun + 은/는 (1)
- ☐ Asking nationality
- ☐ noun 1 + 은/는 + noun 2 + 이/가 아니에요
- ☐ Job & Country
- ☐ noun + 이에요/예요
- ☐ 어느 + noun
- ☐ Answering to the question
- ☐ How to Address People in Korean

Lesson 01

한글

Hangul

Vowels (1)

In the Korean language, every syllable has one or two vowels.

★ Single Vowels

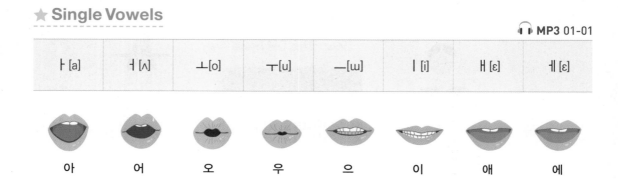

ㅏ [a]	ㅓ [ʌ]	ㅗ [o]	ㅜ [u]	ㅡ [ɯ]	ㅣ [i]	ㅐ [ɛ]	ㅔ [ɛ]
아	어	오	우	으	이	애	에

Difficult Vowel Sounds for Non-native Speakers

The hardest vowels to pronounce in the Korean language are [ㅓ], [ㅜ], [ㅗ] and [ㅡ]. When you pronounce [ㅜ] and [ㅗ], round your lips and stick out your lips as much as you can. The back of the tongue is higher for [ㅜ] than for [ㅗ]. When you move from the sound [ㅗ] to the sound [ㅡ], make your lips spread and unrounded. When you move from the sound [ㅜ] to the sound [ㅓ], lower your jaw and make your lips relaxed and slightly parted.

★ Diphthongs (1)

ㅑ [ja]	ㅕ [jʌ]	ㅛ [jo]	ㅠ [ju]	ㅒ [jɛ]	ㅖ [jɛ]

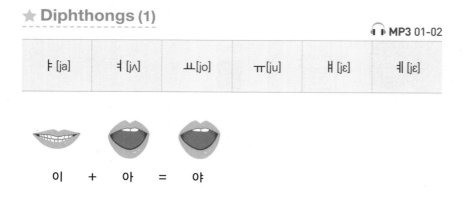

이 + 아 = 야

A double vowel, or a diphthong, is a combination of two vowel sounds. It begins as one vowel and ends as the other. Therefore, the shape of your mouth changes while you're pronouncing a diphthong. For example, when pronouncing [ㅑ], your articulators glide from the semivowel [ㅣ] to the vowel [ㅏ]. During the production of a diphthong, the semivowel [ㅣ] usually is shorter than the following vowel.

Consonants (1)

When you pronounce consonants, you should be careful with the shape of your mouth and lips, the position of your tongue and teeth, and the vibration of the vocal cords. A consonant alone can form neither a syllable nor a sound. Most of the consonants are voiceless but the consonants between two vowels are often voiced.

★ Basic consonants (1)

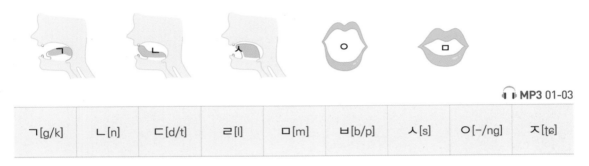

🎧 MP3 01-03

ㄱ[g/k]	ㄴ[n]	ㄷ[d/t]	ㄹ[l]	ㅁ[m]	ㅂ[b/p]	ㅅ[s]	ㅇ[–/ng]	ㅈ[tɕ]

When you write the consonants 'ㅅ', 'ㅈ', and 'ㅊ', the stroke on the left should be longer than that on the right. Also, be careful with the angle of the first stroke of the consonants 'ㅊ' and 'ㅎ'.

★ Basic consonants (2)

🎧 MP3 01-04

ㅊ[tɕʰ]	ㅋ[kʰ]	ㅌ[tʰ]	ㅍ[pʰ]	ㅎ[h]

The consonants [ㅊ], [ㅋ], [ㅌ], [ㅍ], and [ㅎ] have the same tongue positions as the consonants [ㅈ], [ㄱ], [ㄷ], [ㅂ], and [ㅇ], but [ㅊ], [ㅋ], [ㅌ], [ㅍ], and [ㅎ] are more strongly aspirated.

Combination of consonants and vowels (1)

In order to have a sound, every consonant must be combined with a vowel. Each consonant is written differently according to which vowel is combined with it. Write the words down on your worksheet and say them aloud.

ㄱ + ㅏ = 가

	ㄱ	ㄴ	ㄷ	ㄹ	ㅁ	ㅂ	ㅅ	ㅇ	ㅈ	ㅊ	ㅋ	ㅌ	ㅍ	ㅎ
ㅏ	가													
ㅑ	갸													
ㅓ	거													
ㅕ	겨													
ㅗ	고													
ㅛ	교													
ㅜ	구													
ㅠ	규													
ㅡ	그													
ㅣ	기													

If a word starts with a vowel, don't forget to write the open consonant 'ㅇ' before the vowel. Also, when the horizontal vowel 'ㅗ' or 'ㅜ' is combined with the vertical vowel 'ㅏ, ㅐ, ㅓ, ㅔ' or 'ㅣ', be careful about their combining forms.

Vowels (2)

Here are diphthongs combined with semivowel [w], which you should pronounce with your lips rounded.

NOTE When you pronounce [ㅢ], you should make your lips unrounded.

★ Diphthongs (2)

🎧 MP3 01-05

ㅘ[wa]	ㅙ[we]	ㅚ[we]	ㅝ[wʌ]	ㅞ[we]	ㅟ[wi]	ㅢ[ɰi]

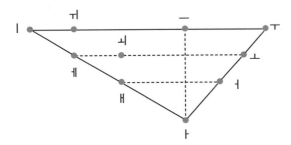

오 + 아 = 와

Difficult Vowel Sounds for Non-native Speakers

The double vowels 'ㅚ', 'ㅙ', and 'ㅞ' look different but have the same sound. Most people tend to say the sound [ㅚ] differently from [ㅙ] and [ㅞ], but you don't need to. There is one more thing to remember. When you write 'ㅞ' or 'ㅝ', be careful that the short stroke of 'ㅔ' or 'ㅓ' is placed under the horizontal stroke of 'ㅜ'. The diphthong [ㅢ] is another difficult vowel sound to say.

★ Double consonants

🎧 ▶ MP3 01-06

ㄲ[k*]	ㄸ[t*]	ㅃ[p*]	ㅆ[s*]	ㅉ[tɕ*]

The double consonants – 'ㄲ, ㄸ, ㅃ, ㅆ' and 'ㅉ' – originate from their basic counterparts – 'ㄱ, ㄷ, ㅂ, ㅅ' and 'ㅈ'. The pronunciation of the double consonants is nearly the same as the pronunciation of their basic counterparts. However, when you pronounce the double consonants, you should tighten your throat muscle a little more.

The sounds of [ㄱ], [ㄷ], [ㅂ], [ㅅ] and [ㅈ] become different depending on whether they are at the beginning or at the end of a word. The sounds of [ㅋ], [ㅌ], [ㅍ] and [ㅊ] are similar to those of their basic counterparts – [ㄱ], [ㄷ], [ㅂ] and [ㅈ] –, but they are more strongly aspirated. The sounds of [ㄲ], [ㄸ], [ㅃ], [ㅆ] and [ㅉ] will make your throat muscle feel tenser than their counterparts. When you're pronouncing [ㅆ], blow out air longer than when pronouncing [ㅅ].

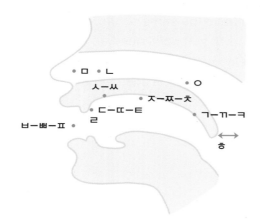

Batchim (1)

You've learned how consonants combine with vowels. I'm sure you know a syllable is made up of either a vowel or the combination of a vowel and consonants. Korean syllables are mainly categorized into three: V (open consonant ㅇ–vowel), CV (consonant–vowel), and CVC (consonant–vowel–consonant). In the Korean language, 14 basic consonants and several double consonants can be used as a batchim, which is the final consonant of a Korean syllable, but each batchim is pronounced with one of seven different sounds: [ㄱ], [ㄴ], [ㄷ], [ㄹ], [ㅁ], [ㅂ], and [ㅇ]. When you pronounce a syllable with a batchim, your mouth should be closed at the end.

🎧 **MP3 01-07**

악[악]	안[안]	앝[앋]	알[알]	암[암]	압[압]	앗[앋]
앙[앙]	앚[앋]	앛[앋]	앜[악]	앝[앋]	앞[압]	앟[앋]

When the final consonant of a syllable is 'ㄱ', 'ㄲ', or 'ㅋ', it sounds like [ㄱ]. When the final consonant of a syllable is 'ㄷ, ㅅ, ㅆ, ㅈ, ㅊ' or 'ㅎ', it is pronounced like [ㄷ]. When the final consonant of a syllable is 'ㅂ' or 'ㅍ', it is sounded as [ㅂ]. Note that the final consonant 'ㅎ' before a vowel is silent.

Batchim (2)

So far you've learned about the syllables with one final consonant. However, two consonants can be used in the batchim. Even though two consonants are written only one of them is pronounced.

🎧 **MP3 01-08**

밖[박]	앉다[안따]	않[안]	닭[닥]	여덟[여덜]	밟다[밥따]	앓다[알타]	없다[업따]

 **Lenition**

Lenition in the Korean language is a phonological process where the final consonant in one syllable sounds like the initial consonant of the following syllable that begins with a vowel sound. If there are two final consonants, both of them are voiced, as in '읽어요'[일거요]. If the final consonants are 'ㄶ' or 'ㅀ', 'ㅎ' is silent, such as '많아요'[마나요] and '앓아요'[아라요]. If the final consonant is 'ㄲ' or 'ㅆ', the double consonants are voiced with their usual sound, as in '있어요'[이써요]. However, if the final consonant is 'ㅇ', there is no consonant lenition.

🎧 MP3 01-09

밥을 먹어요[바블 머거요]	교실에 가요[교시레 가요]	꽃을 사요[꼬츨 사요]
*책을 읽어요[채글 일거요]	*가방이 있어요[가방이 이써요]	*기분이 좋아요[기부니 조아요]

Combination of consonants and vowels (2)

So far you've learned about consonants and vowels in the Korean language. Combine consonants and vowels and read them aloud.

ㄱ + ㅏ + ㅆ + ㅇ + ㅓ + ㅇ + ㅛ	갔어요

ㄱ + ㅏ + ㅇ + ㅇ + ㅏ + ㅈ + ㅣ		ㅋ + ㅗ + ㄲ + ㅣ + ㄹ + ㅣ	
ㄴ + ㅜ + ㄴ + ㅏ		ㅌ + ㅣ + ㅋ + ㅔ + ㅅ	
ㄷ + ㅡ + ㄹ + ㅇ + ㅓ + ㅇ + ㅛ		ㅍ + ㅖ + ㅅ + ㅙ	
ㄹ + ㅏ + ㅁ + ㅕ + ㄴ		ㅎ + ㅏ + ㅇ + ㅒ + ㅇ + ㅛ	
ㅁ + ㅣ + ㅇ + ㅛ + ㅇ + ㅅ + ㅣ + ㄹ		ㄲ + ㅡ + ㅌ	
ㅂ + ㅜ + ㅇ + ㅓ + ㅋ		ㄸ + ㅓ + ㄱ + ㄱ + ㅜ + ㄱ	
ㅅ + ㅏ + ㄹ + ㅏ + ㅁ		ㅃ + ㅗ + ㅃ + ㅗ	
ㅇ + ㅞ + ㅇ + ㅣ + ㅌ + ㅓ		ㅆ + ㅡ + ㄹ + ㅔ + ㄱ + ㅣ	
ㅈ + ㅏ + ㅆ + ㅇ + ㅓ + ㅇ + ㅛ		ㅉ + ㅗ + ㄹ + ㅁ + ㅕ + ㄴ	
ㅊ + ㅜ + ㅇ + ㅝ + ㅇ + ㅛ			

Lesson 02

인사 표현

Greetings

🎧 **MP3** 02-01

Tip '안녕하세요' (informal-polite) and '안녕' (informal) are the most commonly used greetings in Korea. We say '안녕하세요' to acquaintances as well as strangers. Normally, we bow low when we say '안녕하세요'. However, when we come across someone we know in an office or in a school, we just slightly nod our head.

🎧 **MP3** 02-02

Tip '안녕' is a casual and friendly greeting among friends. It means both 'hello' and 'goodbye'. Usually, when it is used for hello, it has a rising intonation. Conversely, when it is used for goodbye, it has a falling intonation.

🎧 **MP3** 02-03

Tip When we've just been introduced to someone, we say '만나서 반갑습니다'.

When leaving someone

> **Tip** '안녕히 계세요' (informal-polite) is used when the speaker is leaving and the listener is staying. Conversely, '안녕히 가세요' (informal-polite) is used when the listener is leaving and the speaker is staying.

> **Tip** '잘 있어' (informal) and '잘 가' (informal) are casual and friendly greetings among friends.

> **Tip** '주말 잘 보내세요' means having a great weekend.

Apologizing

🎧 **MP3** 02-07

mi-an-ham-ni-da/joe-song-ham-ni-da
미안합니다./죄송합니다.
I'm sorry.

gwaen-chan-sseum-ni-da
괜찮습니다.
That's all right.

Tip When we need to apologize to someone, we say '죄송합니다' or '미안합니다'. The normal reply is '괜찮습니다'.

Thanking

🎧 **MP3** 02-08

ə-ni-e-yo
아니에요.
My pleasure.

go-map-seum-nida/gam-sa-ham-ni-da
고맙습니다./감사합니다.
Thank you.

Tip '고맙습니다' and '감사합니다' are used to say thank you. The possible replies are '뭘요, 별거 아니에요, 신경 쓰지 마세요, 아니에요, etc'.

Congratulating

🎧 **MP3** 02-09

chu-ka-ham-ni-da
축하합니다.
Congratulations.

go-map-seum-ni-da
고맙습니다.
Thank you.

Tip When we want to congratulate someone on his or her wedding, birthday, promotion, etc., we say '축하합니다'. The normal replies are '고맙습니다' and '감사합니다'. In this situation, you cannot say '아니에요' when you hear '고맙습니다'.

When going out

🎧 **MP3** 02-10

da-nyeo-o-get-seum-ni-da
다녀오겠습니다.
See you later.

jal-da-nyeo-o-se-yo
잘 다녀오세요.
Bye. Have a nice day.

When coming home

🎧 **MP3** 02-11

da-nyeo-owat-seum-ni-da
다녀왔습니다.
I'm home. / I'm back.

When visiting someone

🎧 **MP3** 02-12

ne, deul-eo-o-se-yo
네, 들어오세요.
Come in.

sil-lye-ham-ni-da
실례합니다.
Excuse me.

Tip When we visit someone, we say '실례합니다'. You should go in after you hear the host say '들어오세요'.

When asking about health, etc.

🎧 MP3 02-13

jəl-ji-nae-se-yo
잘 지내세요?
How is it going?

ne, jəl-ji-nae-yo
네, 잘 지내요.
I'm great.

Tip When we encounter an acquaintance, we usually say '안녕하세요' followed by '잘 지내세요?'. The normal replay is '잘 지내요'.

o-raen-man-i-e-yo
오랜만이에요.
Long time no see.

o-rae-gan-ma-ni-e-yo
오래간만이에요.
Long time no see.

Tip When we meet someone we haven't seen for a long time, we say '오랜만이에요' or '오래간만이에요'.

Before/after meals

Before meals

🎧 MP3 02-14

jəl-meok-get-seum-ni-da
잘 먹겠습니다.
Thank you for the meal.

After meals

jəl-meo-geot-seum-ni-da
잘 먹었습니다.
I really enjoyed the meal.

Tip '잘 먹겠습니다' and '잘 먹었습니다' have different meanings. When we're about to start eating, we say '잘 먹겠습니다'. Conversely, when we finish eating, we say '잘 먹었습니다'.

When going to bed

🎧 MP3 02-15

an-nyeong-hi-ju-mu-se-yo
안녕히 주무세요.
Good night.

jal-ja
잘 자.
Good night.

Tip When going to bed, we say '잘 자' to people of the same age of us and to people who are younger than us. Parents also say '잘 자' to their little children. You cannot say '잘 자' to older people. It sounds very impolite. To older people you should say '안녕히 주무세요'.

❓ When asking a question to stranger

🎧 MP3 02-16

sil-lye-ham-ni-da
실례합니다.
Excuse me.

Tip We say '실례합니다' before we ask a stranger for directions or when we have a question to ask of someone. When we get off the crowded subway, bus, or elevator, etc., we can also say '실례합니다'.

New Year Greetings

🎧 MP3 02-17

sae-hae-bok-ma-ni-ba-deu-se-yo
새해 복 많이 받으세요.
Happy New Year!

Tip At the beginning of the year, we say '새해 복 많이 받으세요' to everyone we meet.

Lesson 03

저는 투이예요.

I'm Thuy.

Key Sentences

1

an-nyeong-ha-se-yo   jeo-neun-dong-hyeo-ni-e-yo

A 안녕하세요? 저는 동현이에요. Hello. I'm Donghyun.

an-nyeong-ha-se-yo   jeo-neun-tu-i-ye-yo

B 안녕하세요? 저는 투이예요. Hello. I'm Thuy.

★ noun + 은/는 (1)

'은/는' is used to mark the topic of the sentence or conversation. If the noun has a batchim in the last letter, you add '은' after the noun, but if it doesn't have a batchim and ends in a vowel, you add '는'.

명사 받침 (O) + 은	명사 받침 (X) + 는
마이클 → 마이클은	저 → 저는

ex 제 이름은 투이예요. My name is Thuy.

저는 투이예요. I'm Thuy.

★ noun + 이에요/예요

If you add '이에요/예요' to a noun, you are identifying something as the noun. If the noun has a batchim in the last letter, you add '이에요' after the noun, but if it doesn't have a batchim and ends in a vowel, you add '예요'.

명사 받침 (O) + 이에요	명사 받침 (X) + 예요
학생 → 학생이에요	기자 → 기자예요

ex 저는 학생이에요. I'm a student.

마이클은 의사예요. Michael is a doctor.

Reviews

❶ 민수 씨_____ 의사_____. Minsu is a doctor.

❷ 양양_____ 경찰_____. Yangyang is a policeman.

Tips

A Korean name consists of a family name followed by a given name. When you should address someone, you can say OO씨, adding a title 씨 to the end of his or her given name. You cannot call someone who is older than yourself OO씨. It sounds very impolite.

Vocabulary

저는 I'm
제 이름 my name
학생 student
기자 reporter
의사 doctor
경찰 policeman

Answers

① 는/예요 ② 은/이에요

2

tu-i-ssi-neun-eo-neu-na-ra-sa-ra-mi-e-yo

A 투이 씨는 어느 나라 사람이에요?
Where are you from, Thuy?

jeo-neun-be-teu-nam-sa-ra-mi-e-yo

B 저는 베트남 사람이에요. I'm Vietnamese.

★ Asking nationality

When we ask someone about his or her nationality, we say '어느 나라 사람이에요?' or '어느 나라에서 왔어요?'. The possible replies are '저는 베트남 사람이에요' (meaning 'I'm a Vietnamese') and '저는 베트남에서 왔어요' (meaning 'I'm from Vietnam').

ex A: 투이 씨는 어느 나라에서 왔어요? What country are you from?
   B: 저는 베트남에서 왔어요. I'm from Vietnam.

★ 어느 + noun

Before nouns, '어느' (meaning 'which') can be used to ask questions where there are two or more possible answers or alternatives.

ex 투이 씨는 어느 학교 학생이에요? Which school do you study at?
   우리 교실은 어느 교실이에요? Which classroom is our classroom?

Tips

Since in the Korean language a declarative sentence has the same word order as its interrogative counterpart, you may find it difficult to distinguish them. Usually, the declarative sentence has nearly flat intonation, with a fall in pitch at the end. The interrogative sentence rises at the end.

ex 안녕하세요?
   (rise at the end)
   안녕하세요.
   (fall at the end)

Vocabulary

어느 which
나라 country
베트남 Vietnam
학교 school
학생 student
우리 our
교실 classroom

Reviews

❶ 민수 씨는 _____이에요? Minsu, where are you from?

❷ 양양 씨는 _____에서 왔어요?
   Yangyang, where are you come from?

Answers

① 어느 나라 사람 ② 어느 나라

Key Sentences

3

dong-hyeon-ssi-neun-yu-hak-saeng-i-e-yo

A 동현 씨는 유학생이에요?   Are you an international student, Donghyun?

a-ni-yo   (jeo-neun)-yu-hak-saeng-i-a-ni-e-yo

B 아니요. (저는) 유학생이 아니에요.
No, (I) am not an international student.

★ noun 1 + 은/는 + noun 2 + 이/가 아니에요

When we want to say 『Noun 1 is not Noun 2』, we use the 『Noun 1 + 은/
는 + Noun 2 + 이/가 아니에요.』 structure. '아니에요' is the negative form of
'이에요/예요'. Which marker comes after the noun depends on whether
the last syllable of the noun has a batchim or not. That is, when the
noun has a batchim in the last syllable, we add '은' or '이', but when it
doesn't have a batchim and ends in a vowel, we add '는' or '가'.

명사 받침 (O) + 이 아니에요	명사 받침 (X) + 가 아니에요
학생 → 학생이 아니에요	기자 → 기자가 아니에요

ex 저는 미국 사람이 아니에요. I'm not American.
양양은 의사가 아니에요. Yangyang is not a doctor.

★ Answering to the question

We answer '네' or '아니요' to yes/no questions. '네' is a positive
answer and '아니요' is a negative answer.

ex **A:** 투이 씨는 베트남 사람이에요? Thuy, are you Vietnamese?
B: 네. / 아니요. Yes. (I am Vietnamese.) / No. (I am not Vietnamese.)

Reviews

❶ 민수 씨_____ 의사_____ 아니에요.   Minsu is not a doctor.

❷ 양양은 일본 사람_____.   Yangyang is not a Japanese.

Tips

In the Korean language,
not every sentence needs
a subject. Unlike English, if
everyone will know what the
speaker means, the subject
can be left out.

ex A 투이 씨는 베트남 사람이에
요?
B 네, 베트남 사람이에요. /
아니요, 베트남 사람이 아
니에요.

Vocabulary

유학생 international
  student
아니요 no
네 yes
학생 student
기자 reporter
미국 사람 American
의사 doctor
베트남 사람 Vietnamese
일본 사람 Japanese

Answers

① 는/가 ② 이 아니에요

38

Job & Country

[seon-saeng-nim]
선생님
teacher

[hoe-sa-won]
회사원
employee

[hak-saeng]
학생
student

[un-dong-seon-su]
운동선수
athlete

[ui-sa]
의사
doctor

[gi-ja]
기자
reporter

[han-guk]
한국
Korea

[jung-guk]
중국
China

[il-bon]
일본
Japan

[be-teu-nam]
베트남
Vietnam

[mi-guk]
미국
the United States

[kae-na-da]
캐나다
Canada

Dialog

MP3 03-08 ✎ MP3 03-09

ən-nyeong-hə-se-yo jeo-neun-dong-hyeo-ni-e-yo
안녕하세요? 저는 동현이에요.

ən-nyeong-hə-se-yo jeo-neun-tu-i-ye-yo
안녕하세요? 저는 투이예요.

tu-i-ssi-neun-eo-neu-nə-rə-e-seo-owə-sseo-yo
투이 씨는 어느 나라에서 왔어요?

jeo-neun-be-teu-nəm-e-seo-owə-sseo-yo
저는 베트남에서 왔어요.

tu-i-ssi-neun-yu-hək-sæng-i-e-yo
투이 씨는 유학생이에요?

ne   (jeo-neun)-yu-hək-sæng-i-e-yo
네, (저는) 유학생이에요.

dong-hyeo-ssi-do-yu-hək-sæng-i-e-yo
동현 씨도 유학생이에요?

ə-ni-yo   jeo-neun-yu-hək-sæng-i-ə-ni-e-yo
아니요. 저는 유학생이 아니에요.

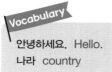

안녕하세요. Hello.	저는 I'm	어느 which
나라 country	유학생 international student	

40

Donghyun	Hello. I'm Donghyun.
Thuy	Hello. I'm Thuy.
Donghyun	Where are you from, Thuy?
Thuy	I'm from Vietnam.
Donghyun	Are you an international college student?
Thuy	Yes, (I) am an international student.
	Are you an international student, too, Donghyun?
Donghyun	No. I'm not an international student.

1 **Fill in the blanks and say the sentences aloud.**

1 _____ 마이클이에요. I'm Michael.

2 민수 씨는 _____? Minsu, are you a student?

3 양양___ 회사원___ 아니에요. Yangyang doesn't work for a company.

2 **Unscramble the words in order to make a sentence.**

1 [학생 / 이에요 / 마이클 / 은] Michael is a student.

→ _____

2 [어느 / 사람 / 나라 / 이에요?] Where are you from?

→ _____

3 [저 / 가 / 는 / 의사 / 아니에요] I'm not a doctor.

→ _____

4 [일본 / 에서 / 도모코 씨 / 는 / 왔어요] Domoko is from Japan.

→ _____

 Answers **1** 1. 저는 2. 학생이에요 3. 은/이
2 1. 마이클은 학생이에요. 2. 어느 나라 사람이에요? 3. 저는 의사가 아니에요. 4. 도모코 씨는 일본에서 왔어요.

How to Address People in Korean

As you've learned earlier, you can call people 『the person's given name + 씨』. If you don't know the given name, you can say '저기요'. This expression is used when you need to get someone's attention, for example, when you ask a passerby for directions, when you call the waiter in a restaurant or in a café to order something, or when you want to let someone know that he or she dropped something.

Lesson 04

이거는 뭐예요?

What's this?

Scan the QR code

Super Easy Korean
for Beginners:
A Self-study Book

Lesson 03

Lesson 04

Video Lectures   Videos for Reviewing

MP3 for Listening   Videos for Words

Lesson 05

Lesson 06

Study Plan

Video Lectures

Book

Videos for Reviewing

Word Lists

Videos for Words

Key Sentences

1

dong-hyeon-ssi i-geo-neun-mwo-ye-yo

A 동현 씨, 이거는 뭐예요? Donghyun, what's this?

i-geon-han-gu-geo-chae-gi-e-yo

B 이건 한국어 책이에요. This is a Korean book.

⭐ 이것, 저것, and 그것

'이것' (meaning 'this'), '저것' (meaning 'that') and '그것' (meaning 'it') are pronouns that refer to things. '이거', '저거' and '그거' are the informal way of saying these words, but they are more widely used.

ex 이거는(= 이것은) 가방이에요. This is a bag.
저거는(= 저것은) 펜이에요. That is a pen.
그거는(= 그것은) 지우개예요. It is an eraser.

⭐ 뭐/무엇

When we want to ask about a thing or fact, we say '뭐예요?', which is a short form of '무엇이에요?'. In everyday speech, we normally use '뭐' (informal) rather than '무엇' (formal). However, we use '무엇' in writing.

ex **A:** 이름이 뭐예요?(= 무엇이에요?) What is your name?
B: 제 이름은 동현이에요. My name is Donghyeon.
A: 직업이 뭐예요? What is your job?
B: 저는 선생님이에요. I am a teacher.

 Tips

In speech, Korean people normally use short forms. Full forms are '이것은 / 저것은', short forms are '이건 / 저건'.

ex 이거는 가방이에요.
= 이건 가방이에요.

저거는 펜이에요.
= 저건 펜이에요.

그거는 지우개예요.
= 그건 지우개예요.

 Vocabulary

책 book
가방 bag
펜 pen
지우개 eraser
직업 job
선생님 teacher
핸드폰 cellular phone
시계 watch

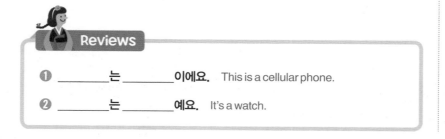 **Reviews**

❶ _____는 _____이에요. This is a cellular phone.

❷ _____는 _____예요. It's a watch.

 Answers

① 이거/휴대폰 ② 그거/시계

2

i-geon-nu-gu-ui-chae-gi-ye-yo

A 이건 누구의 책이에요?　Whose book is this?

geu-geon-ma-i-keul-ssi-ui-chae-gi-ye-yo

B 그건 마이클 씨의 책이에요.　It's Michael's book.

★ noun + 의 + noun

'의' between two nouns shows ownership or possession. '의' is similar to the preposition of possession 'of' in English. For example, '마이클 씨의 책' (meaning 'a book of Michael') means the book belongs to Michael.

ex 양양 씨의 집　Yangyang's house

　　마이클 씨의 책　Michael's book

　　동현 씨의 휴대폰　Donghyun's cellular phone

★ 누구

When we want to ask about a person or a group of people, we use '누구' (meaning 'who'). On the other hand, when we want to ask about a thing or fact, we use '무엇' (meaning 'what').

ex A: 누구예요?　Who is she?

　　B: 제 친구 양양이에요.　She is my friend, Yangyang.

Tips

Here is a list of contractions.

· Contraction: 제 / 네 / 내

· Meaning: 저의 / 너의 / 나의

These contractions are more commonly used in speech because they sound more natural.

ex 이건 내 책이에요.
This is my book.

그건 네 책이 아니야.
That is not your book.

Vocabulary

책　book

집　house

친구　friend

공책　notebook

Reviews

❶ 그건 _____의 휴대폰이에요? / 제 거예요.

Whose cellular phone is it? / It's mine.

❷ 이거는 마이클 씨의 공책이에요? / 아니요. _____거예요.

Is this Michael's notebook? / No, it's Linda's.

Answers

① 누구　② 린다 씨의

🎧 **MP3** 04-05 🎤 **MP3** 04-06

3

i-gong-chae-geun-je-ggeo-ye-yo

A 이 공책은 제 거예요? Is this notebook mine?

a-ni-yo   geu-gong-chaek-do-ma-i-keul-ssi-ui-gge-ye-yo

B 아니요, 그 공책도 마이클 씨의 거예요.
No, the notebook is also Micheal's.

★ 이/그/저＋noun

'이' (meaning 'this'), '그' (meaning 'the'), and '저' (meaning 'that') can be used as determiners before noun. We use '이' for a person or an object that is close to the speaker, while we use '저' for a person or an object that is far from both the speaker and the listener. We use '그' for a person or an object that is not close to the speaker but is close to the listener.

ex 이 사람은 우리 반 친구예요. This is my classmate.
저 집은 마이클 씨의 집이에요. That house is Michael's.
그 학교는 우리 학교가 아니에요. It is not my school.

★ noun＋도

Use '–도' (meaning 'also' or 'too') when you want to talk about a person or object that has the same characteristic as another person or object.

ex **A:** 저는 미국에서 왔어요. I'm from America.
B: 저도 미국에서 왔어요. I'm from America, too.

Reviews

❶ _____ 공책은 양양 씨의 공책이 아니에요.
That notebook is not Yangyang's notebook.

❷ 저는 학생이에요. 동현 씨_____ 학생이에요. 우리는 학생이에요.
I'm a student. Donghyun is a student, too. We are students.

Tips

1. '그것' or '그거' is used to indicate an object that has been previously mentioned.

2. '도' can be used as a subject marker just like '은/는/이/가'. Be careful not to use '도' with '은/는/이/가', for example '이 책은도' and '저 지우개는도'.

3. We also use '그' to indicate a person or an object previously mentioned that is not in the presence of either speaker or the listener at the time of speaking.

Vocabulary

공책 notebook
반 친구 classmate
학교 school
미국 America

Answers

① 저 ② 도

48

Classroom Stuff

[chil-pan]
칠판
blackboard

[ui-ja]
의자
chair

[chaek-ssang]
책상
desk

[chaek]
책
book

[gong-chaek]
공책
notebook

[bolpen(pen)]
볼펜(펜)
ballpoint (pen)

[pil-tong]
필통
pencil case

[yeon-pil]
연필
pencil

[ge-si-pan]
게시판
bulletin board

[ji-u-gae]
지우개
eraser

[no-teu-buk]
노트북
laptop

[si-gye]
시계
clock

Dialog

🎧 MP3 04-08 🎤 MP3 04-09

dong-hyeon-ssi i-geon-mwo-ye-yo
동현 씨, 이건 뭐예요?

geu-geon-han-gu-geo-chae-gi-ye-yo
그건 한국어 책이에요.

i-geon-nu-gu-ui-chae-gi-ye-yo
이건 누구의 책이에요?

geu-geo-neun-ma-i-keul-ssi-ui-geo-ye-yo
그거는 마이클 씨의 거예요.

geu-reom jeo-geo-neun-je-chae-gi-ye-yo
그럼, 저거는 제 책이에요?

a-ni-yo   jeo-geot-tto-ma-i-keul-ssi-ui-geo-ye-yo
아니요. 저것도 마이클 씨의 거예요.

tu-i-ssi-ui-chae-geun-i-geo-ye-yo
투이 씨의 책은 이거예요.

ne   al-ge-sseo-yo-go-ma-wo-yo
네, 알겠어요. 고마워요.

a-ni-e-yo
아니에요.

Vocabulary

이거(이것) this	그거(그것) it	한국어 책 Korean book
누구의 whose	그럼 then	저거(저것) that

Thuy	Donghyun, what's this?
Donghyun	It's a Korean book.
Thuy	Whose book is this?
Donghyun	It's Michael's.
Thuy	Then, is that book mine?
Donghyun	No. That's Michael's, too. Yours are here.
Thuy	Okay. Thank you.
Donghyun	My pleasure.

Exercises

1 Fill in the blanks and say the sentences aloud.

1 _____는 제 _____이에요. This is my cellular phone.

2 _____은 _____의 책이에요? Whose book is it?

3 _____은 마이클___가방이에요. That is Michael's bag.

2 Unscramble the words in order to make a sentence.

1 [선생님 / 이에요 / 양양 / 도] Yangyang is a teacher, too.

→ _____

2 [누구 / 친구 / 의 / 예요?] Whose friend are you?

→ _____

3 [는 / 가 / 이거 / 의자 / 아니에요] This is not a chair.

→ _____

4 [이름이 / 뭐 / 예요 / 이 / 남자 / 의] What is this guy's name?

→ _____

Answers   1   1. 이거/휴대폰   2. 그것/누구   3. 저것/의
          2   1. 양양도 선생님이에요.   2. 누구의 친구예요?   3. 이거는 의자가 아니에요.   4. 이 남자의 이름이 뭐예요?

What the Word "our" Means to the Korean People

Two people are talking to each other.

"Our husband works for a company." says Person A.

"Our husband is a doctor." says Person B.

In the dialog above "our husband" doesn't make sense because my husband and your husband cannot be the same person. However, Korean people normally say '우리' instead of '내' or '나의' even though they know it is grammatically incorrect. This is because they have a strong community spirit.

Lesson 05

학생 식당이
어디에 있어요?

Where is the students' cafeteria?

Scan the QR code

Super Easy Korean
for Beginners:
A Self-study Book

Lesson 04

Lesson 05

Video Lectures   Videos for Reviewing

MP3 for Listening   Videos for Words

Lesson 06

Lesson 07

Study Plan

Video Lectures

Book

Videos for Reviewing

Word Lists

Videos for Words

Key Sentences

1

A
dong-hyeon-ssi   eo-di-e-ga-yo
동현 씨, 어디에 가요? Donghyun, where are you going?

B
hak-saeng-sik-dang-e-ga-yo
학생 식당에 가요. I'm going to the students' cafeteria.

★ **place + 에 가요/있어요/없어요**

We use 『place + 에』 to describe the direction or location of a place. We also use this pattern to describe where someone or something is. 『place + 에 있어요』 means someone or something exists somewhere. '있어요' means to exist somewhere, while '없어요' means not to exist somewhere.

ex 저는 회사에 가요. I am going to company.
마이클은 집에 있어요. Michael is at home.
동현 씨는 학교에 없어요. Donghyeon is not in the school.

★ **어디**

When you want to ask about a place, use '어디' (meaning 'where').

ex 여기가 어디예요? Where are we?
어디에 가요? Where are you going?
마이클은 어디에 있어요? Where is Michael?

 Tips

'있어요' and '없어요' can also be used to talk about whether or not you have something or someone, for example, '저는 아들이 있어요' (meaning 'I have a son').

ex 저는 휴대 전화가 있어요.
I have a cellular phone.
양양은 한국 친구가 없어요.
Yangyang doesn't have Korean friends.

 Vocabulary

학생 식당 students' cafeteria
회사 work
집 home
학교 school
방 room

 **Reviews**

❶ _____에 가요? Are you going to work?

❷ 휴대폰이 _____에 있어요? / _____에 있어요.
Where is my cellular phone? / It's in the room.

Answers

① 회사 ② 어디/방

2

hak-saeng-sik-dang-i-eo-di-e-i-sseo-yo

A 학생 식당이 어디에 있어요?
Where is the students' cafeteria?

jeo-geon-mul-yeo-pe-i-sseo-yo

B 저 건물 옆에 있어요. It's next to that building.

⭐ noun + 이/가

When '이' or '가' is added to a noun, it makes the noun a subject.

명사 받침 (O) + 이	명사 받침 (X) + 가
학생 식당 → 학생 식당이	학교 → 학교가
공원 → 공원이	휴대 전화 → 휴대 전화가

ex 마이클이 집에 있어요. Michael is at home.

우리 집 근처에 학교가 있어요. There is a school near my house.

⭐ Expressing location

If you want to say where someone or something is, you can use a structure with 「noun + 의 + location + 에 있어요/없어요」. The particle '의', which shows ownership, can be left out.

ex 공원 앞에 학교가 있어요. There is a school in front of the park.

책상 위에 가방이 있어요. There is a bag on the desk.

Reviews

❶ 지갑이 어디에 있어요? / 책상 _____에 있어요.
Where is the wallet? / It's on the desk.

❷ 공원이 어디에 있어요? / 집 _____에 있어요.
Where is the park? / It's in front of the house.

 Tips

When someone or something is located at a short distance from you, you can use the word '근처' (meaning 'nearby').

ex 학교 근처에 공원이 있어요.
There is a park nearby school.

 Vocabulary

학생 식당 students' cafeteria
건물 building
근처 near
공원 park
앞 in front of
책상 desk
위 on
가방 bag
지갑 wallet

Answers

① 위 ② 앞

🎧 MP3 05-05 🎤 MP3 05-06

3

yeo-gi-ga-hak-saeng-sik-dang-i-e-yo

A 여기가 학생 식당이에요? Is this a students' cafeteria?

a-ni-yo   hak-saeng-sik-dang-eun-jeo-gi-e-i-sseo-yo

B 아니요. 학생 식당은 저기에 있어요.
No. The students' cafeteria is over there.

★ 여기, 거기 and 저기

'여기' (meaning 'here'), '거기' (meaning 'there'), and '저기' (meaning 'over there')
are pronouns used for places.

ex 여기가 우리 집이에요. Here is my house.
거기에 제 친구가 있어요. My friend is there.
저기에 제 책이 있어요. My book is over there.

★ noun + 은/는 (2)

'은/는' is a topic marker. We use it to show that we are talking about
a particular thing or person that has already been mentioned.

명사 받침 (O) + 은	명사 받침 (X) + 는
학생 식당 → 학생 식당은	학교 → 학교는

ex **A:** 마이클 씨가 학교에 있어요? Is Michael at school?
B: 아니요. 마이클 씨는 집에 있어요. No. Michael is at home.

Reviews

❶ 휴대 전화가 어디에 있어요? / _____에 있어요.
Where is the cellular phone? / Here it is.

❷ 저기가 커피숍이에요? / 아니요. 저기____ 식당이에요.
Is that a coffee shop? / No, it's a restaurant.

Tips

The subject is normally put at
the beginning of a sentence,
but adverbials can come
before the subject. However,
when 「a noun +은/는」 is used
as the subject, you cannot put
adverbials at the beginning of a
sentence.

Vocabulary

여기 here
학생 식당 cafeteria
저기 there
집 house
친구 friend
책 book
학교 school
커피숍 coffee shop
식당 restaurant

Answers

① 여기 ② 는

Direction and Location

🎧 MP3 05-07

[wi]
위
on

[a-rae]
아래(= 밑)
under

[an]
안
in

[bak]
밖
out

[yeop]
옆
next to

[ap]
앞
in front of

[dwi]
뒤
behind

[o-reun-jjok]
오른쪽
right

[oen-jjok]
왼쪽
left

Dialog

🎧 MP3 05-08 🎤 MP3 05-09

dong-hyeon-ssi hak-saeng-sik-dang-i-eo-di-e-i-sseo-yo
동현 씨, 학생 식당이 어디에 있어요?

hak-saeng-sik-dang-eun-jeo-geon-mul-yeo-pe-i-sseo-yo
학생 식당은 저 건물 옆에 있어요.

ne   go-ma-wo-yo
네, 고마워요.

a-ni-e-yo   hak-saeng-sik-dang-e-ga-yo
아니에요. 학생 식당에 가요?

ne, dong-hyeon-ssi-neun-eo-di-ga-yo
네, 동현 씨는 어디 가요?

jeo-neun-do-seo-gwan-e-ga-yo
저는 도서관에 가요.

geu-rae-yo   an-nyeong-hi-ga-se-yo
그래요? 안녕히 가세요.

ne, tu-i-ssi-do-yo
네, 투이 씨도요.

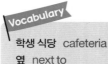

학생 식당 cafeteria	어디 where	건물 building
옆 next to	도서관 library	

Thuy	Donghyun, where is the students' cafeteria?
Donghyun	The students' cafeteria is next to that building.
Thuy	Okay. Thank you.
Donghyun	You're welcome. Are you going to the students' cafeteria?
Thuy	Yes. Where are you going, Donghyun?
Donghyun	I'm going to the library.
Thuy	Are you? Okay. Bye.
Donghyun	Bye.

1 **Fill in the blanks and say the sentences aloud.**

1 여기가 제 ____이에요. This is my room.

2 책상 ____에 가방이 있어요. There is a bag on the desk.

3 가방 ____에 책이 있어요. There is a book in the bag.

4 필통은 방에 _____. The pencil case is not in the room.

2 **Unscramble the words in order to make a sentence.**

1 [화장실 / 이 / 에 / 있어요 / 어디] Where is the bathroom?

→ _____

2 [우리 / 근처 / 집 / 공원 / 이 / 에 / 있어요] There is a park near my house.

→ _____

3 [이 / 마이클 / 학교 / 에 / 가요] Michael is going to school.

→ _____

4 [제 / 여기 / 가 / 방 / 이에요] This is my room.

→ _____

"어디" Where

'어디 가요?' can be used as a greeting. When you come across someone you know, you can say '어디 가요?' instead of '안녕하세요?'. '어디' is used when you want to ask about a place. If you want to say someone is somewhere, you can use 『place + 에 있어요』. Often you can hear some Koreans say '저 화장실이에요' (meaning 'I'm the bathroom'). Of course, this sentence is a grammatically incorrect because a person cannot be a bathroom. However, many Koreans say like this instead of saying '(저는) 화장실에 있어요' (meaning 'I'm in the bathroom). Similarly, they often say '어디예요?' (meaning 'where is?') instead of saying '어디에 있어요?' (meaning 'where are you?').

Lesson 06

지금 뭐 해요?

What are you doing now?

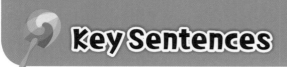
Key Sentences

1

A 투이 씨, 지금 뭐 해요? Thuy, what are you doing now?

B 책을 읽어요. I'm reading a book.

★ verb + -아/어요

In the Korean language, the base form of a verb is '–다'. We add the present tense verb ending '–아/어요' to the verb stem. When the vowel before '–다' is 'ㅏ' or 'ㅗ', add '–아요'. When the vowel before '–다' is not 'ㅏ' or 'ㅗ', add '–어요'. When the base form of a verb ends in '하다', add '여요'. In speech '하여요' is normally contracted to '해요'.

NOTE '듣다' and '쓰다' are irregular verbs.

ㅗ, ㅏ (O) + –아요	ㅗ, ㅏ (X) + –어요	하다 → 해요
살다 → 살아요	먹다 → 먹어요	공부하다 → 공부해요
가다 → 가요	마시다 → 마셔요	운동하다 → 운동해요

★ noun + 을/를 + verb

Many verbs need objects. '을/를' is used to mark the object of a sentence. When the noun has a batchim in the last letter, add '을' but when it doesn't have a batchim and ends in a vowel, add '를'.

명사 받침 (O) + 을	명사 받침 (X) + 를
밥 → 밥을	친구 → 친구를

ex **A:** 무엇을 해요?(= 뭐 해요?) What are you doing?

B: 책을 읽어요. / 편지를 써요.
I'm reading a book. / I'm writing a letter.

 Reviews

❶ 뭐 해요? / 편지_____ 읽어요. What are you doing? / I'm reading a letter.

❷ 뭐 해요?/ 주스_____ 마셔요. What are you doing? / I'm drinking juice.

 Tips

'뭐 해요?' is used to ask what action is taking place, while '뭐예요?' is used to what object it is. '뭐 해요?' and '뭐예요?' sound similar. When you use these expressions, try to say them correctly.

 Vocabulary

지금 now
책 book
읽다 read
살다 live
가다 go
먹다 eat, have
마시다 drink
공부하다 study
운동하다 work out
보다 see
만나다 meet
편지 letter
쓰다 write

 Answers

① 를 ② 를

2

A 어디에서 책을 읽어요? Where do you read books?

B (저는) 도서관에서 책을 읽어요.
I read books in the library.

★ sentence structure: Subject – Object – Verb

In a Korean sentence, the subject normally comes before the object; the verb comes after the object. However, the subject is quite often left out when everyone knows what the subject means. The Korean language has several markers: '은' or '는' is a topic marker, '이' or '가' is a subject marker, and '을' or '를' is an object marker. Meanwhile, some verbs don't need objects, such as '자다' (meaning 'sleep') and '쉬다' (meaning 'rest').

ex 마이클은 자요. Michael is sleeping.
투이 씨는 밥을 먹어요. Thuy is having a meal.

★ place + 에서 + verb

When we talk about a place where an action is occurring, we use 『place +에서』.

ex 저는 집에서 공부해요. I study at home.
투이 씨가 슈퍼마켓(마트/가게)에서 물을 사요. Thuy buys water at supermarket.

Reviews

❶ 어디_____ 편지를 써요? / _____에서 편지를 써요.
Where do you write a letter? / I write a letter at school.

❷ 무엇을 해요? / 가게_____ 빵____ 사요.
What are you doing? / I'm buying some bread.

Answers

① 에서/학교 ② 에서/을

Key Sentences

🎧 MP3 06-05 🎤 MP3 06-06

3

A 재미있어요? Do you enjoy it?

B 네, 그렇지만 조금 어려워요. Yes, but it's a little difficult.

★ adjective + ─아/어요

In speech, the base form of an adjective '─다' changes to '─아요/어요'. The spelling rules for the adjective endings are the same as those for the verb endings. When we ask about the condition of something, we say '어때요' (meaning 'how is it')?

ㅗ, ㅏ (O) + ─아요	ㅗ, ㅏ (X) + ─어요	하다 → 해요
많다 → 많아요	적다 → 적어요	따뜻하다 → 따뜻해요[따뜨태요]
싸다 → 싸요 (싸아요×)	맛없다 → 맛없어요[마덥써요]	시원하다 → 시원해요

ex **A:** 린다 씨, 한국어 공부가 어때요? Linda, how is it going studying Korean?
B: 재미있어요. It's fun.

★ 그리고, 그렇지만, and 그래서

'그리고' (meaning 'and'), '그렇지만' (meaning 'but') and '그래서' (meaning 'so') are used to join sentences.

ex 저는 학생이에요. 그리고 마이클 씨는 선생님이에요.
I'm a student and Michael is a teacher.
한국어 공부는 재미있어요. 그렇지만 어려워요.
Studying Korean is fun but it's difficult.
저는 학생이에요. 그래서 매일 학교에 가요.
I'm a student so I go to school every day.

Reviews

❶ 빵이 싸요. _____ 맛있어요. The bread is cheap and delicious.

❷ 커피가 비싸요. _____ 맛있어요.
The coffee is expensive but delicious.

Tips

1. <'─' 불규칙>
When the adjective/verb stem ends in the vowel '─', leave it out and add '─아/어요'. When the vowel 'ㅏ' or 'ㅗ' comes before the vowel '─', add '─아요' to the stem. When the vowel 'ㅏ' or 'ㅗ' doesn't come, add '─어요'.
ex 아프다 → 아파요
쓰다 → 써요

2. Many verbs and adjective that end with the batchim 'ㅂ' are irregular.
ex 가깝다 → 가까워요
덥다 → 더워요

Vocabulary

재미있다 fun
어렵다 difficult
많다 many, much
싸다 cheap
적다 few, little
따뜻하다 warm
시원하다 cool
매일 every day
맛있다 delicious
비싸다 expensive

Answers

① 그리고 ② 그렇지만

68

Basic verb / adjective

🎧 **MP3** 06-07

★ **Basic verb**

가다 go	**오다** come	**만나다** meet
자다 sleep	**먹다** eat	**읽다** read
마시다 drink	**기다리다** wait	**쓰다** write
운동하다 work out	**전화하다** call	**공부하다** study
보다 watch	**쉬다** take a rest	**일하다** work

★ **Basic adjective**

좋다 ↔ 나쁘다 good ↔ bad	**크다 ↔ 작다** big ↔ small	**많다 ↔ 적다** many, much ↔ few, little
싸다 ↔ 비싸다 cheap ↔ expensive	**재미있다 ↔ 재미없다** fun ↔ not fun	**맛있다 ↔ 맛없다** delicious ↔ not delicious
멋있다 cool	**예쁘다** pretty	**아프다** sick
조용하다 quiet	**피곤하다** tired	**힘들다** hard
덥다 ↔ 춥다 hot ↔ cold	**쉽다 ↔ 어렵다** easy ↔ difficult	**귀엽다** cute

Dialog

🎧 MP3 06-08 🎙 MP3 06-09

 동현 씨, 어디 가요?

 학교에 가요.

 그래요? 학교에서 뭐 해요?

 친구를 만나요. 그리고 도서관에 가요.
투이 씨도 학교에 가요?

 아니요. 저는 영화관에 가요.

 이 근처에 영화관이 있어요?

 아니요. 그렇지만 강남역 근처에 있어요.
그래서 강남역에 가요.

 아~ 그럼 안녕히 가세요. 내일 봐요.

 네, 내일 만나요.

학교 school	친구 friend	그리고 and
도서관 library	영화관 theater	그렇지만 but
강남역 Gangnam station	근처 near	

70

Thuy	Donghyun, where are you going?
Donghyun	I'm going to school.
Thuy	Are you? What are you going to do at school?
Donghyun	I'm going to meet my friends, and go to the library. Are you going to school, too?
Thuy	No. I'm going to the theater.
Donghyun	Is there a theater near here?
Thuy	No. But it is near Gangnam Station. So I'm going to Gangnam Station.
Donghyun	Ahhh.... Then, enjoy the movie. See you tomorrow.
Thuy	See you.

1 **Fill in the blanks and say the sentences aloud.**

1 마이클은 식당_____ 밥을 _____. Michael eats in the dining room.

2 투이 씨는 도서관에서 책____ _____. Thuy reads books in the library.

3 저는 학교에서 한국어___ 공부_____. I study Korean at school.

2 **Unscramble the words in order to make a sentence.**

마이클 커피숍 책을 읽다	양양 공원 운동을 하다	투이 식당 라면을 먹다

1 마이클 씨는 커피숍에서 무엇을 해요? What does Michael do at the coffee shop?

→ _____. Michael reads a book at the coffee shop.

2 양양은 어디에서 운동을 해요? Where does Yangyang work out?

→ _____. Yangyang works out in the park.

3 투이는 식당에서 무엇을 먹어요? What does Thuy eat in the restaurant?

→ _____. Thuy eats ramen in the restaurant.

Answers 　**1** 1.에서/먹어요　2.을/읽어요　3.를/해요
　　　　　2 1. 마이클은 커피숍에서 책을 읽어요.　2. 양양은 공원에서 운동을 해요.　3. 투이는 식당에서 라면을 먹어요.

Different Places and What to Do There

집 home	• 집에서 쉬어요. I take a rest at home. • 텔레비전을 봐요. I watch TV. • 밥을 먹어요. I eat a meal. • 자요. I sleep.
카페 café	• 카페에서 커피를 마셔요. I drink coffee at a café. • 친구를 만나요. I meet my friend.
식당 restaurant	• 식당에서 점심을 먹어요. I eat lunch at a restaurant.
회사 company	• 회사에서 일해요. I work at a company.
도서관 library	• 도서관에서 공부해요. I study at the library. • 책을 읽어요. I read books.
공원 park	• 공원에서 친구를 기다려요. I wait for my friend at the park. • 운동해요. I work out.
백화점 department store	• 백화점에서 옷을 사요. I buy clothes at a department store. • 쇼핑해요. I do shopping.
우체국 post office	• 우체국에서 편지를 보내요. I send a letter at a post office. • 소포를 보내요. I send a parcel.
은행 bank	• 은행에서 돈을 바꿔요. I change some money into won at a bank. • 돈을 찾아요. I withdraw some money. • 돈을 보내요. I wire some money.

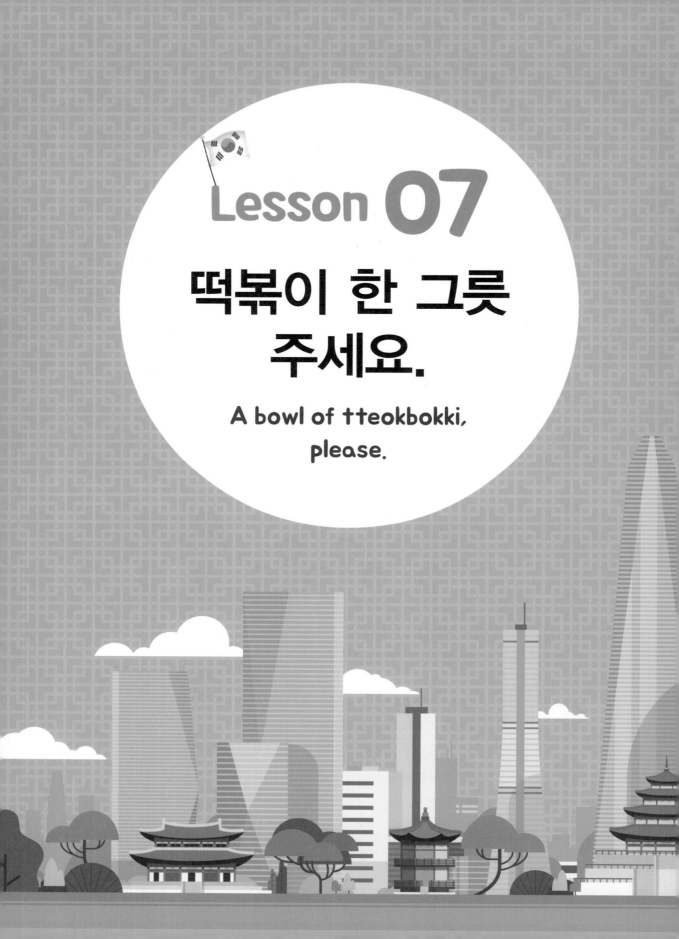

Lesson 07

떡볶이 한 그릇 주세요.

A bowl of tteokbokki, please.

Scan the QR code

Super Easy Korean for Beginners:
A Self-study Book

Lesson 06

Lesson 07

▶ Video Lectures   ⊕ Videos for Reviewing

🔊 MP3 for Listening   📝 Videos for Words

Lesson 08

Lesson 09

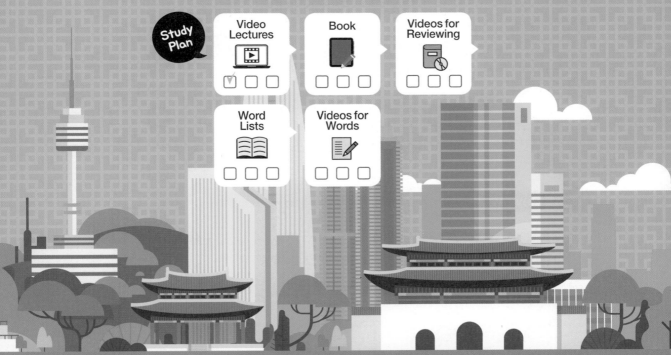

Study Plan

Video Lectures

Book

Videos for Reviewing

Word Lists

Videos for Words

Key Sentences

1

A 투이 씨, 무슨 음식을 먹고 싶어요?
Thuy, what kind of food do you want to eat?

B 저는 한국 음식을 먹고 싶어요.
I'd like to eat Korean food.

★ 무슨 + noun

'무슨' (meaning 'what') is used when there is an undefined set of possibilities for an answer.

ex 무슨 음식을 먹어요? What food are you having?

무슨 노래를 들어요? What song are you listening?

무슨 책을 읽어요? What book are you reading?

★ verb + -고 싶다

When you want to do something, use '-고 싶다' (meaning 'want to' or 'would like to'). Note that the third person cannot be the subject of the sentence that ends in '-고 싶다'.

동사 받침 (O/X) + -고 싶다	
가다 → 가고 싶다	먹다 → 먹고 싶다
쓰다 → 쓰고 싶다	듣다 → 듣고 싶다

ex A: 뭐 하고 싶어요? What do you want to do?

B: 집에서 쉬고 싶어요. I want to take a rest at home.

Reviews

❶ 오늘 뭐 하고 싶어요? / PC방에서 게임을 ＿＿＿＿＿＿.
What do you want to do today? / I want to play games in the Internet café.

❷ ＿＿＿＿＿ 음악을 좋아해요? / 저는 K-pop을 좋아해요.
What kind of music do you like? / I like K-pop.

Tips

If subject is in third person, you should say '-고 싶어 하다' instead of saying '-고 싶다'.

ex 마이클은 비빔밥을 먹고 싶어 해요.
Michael wants to eat bibimbap.

양양은 학교에 가고 싶어 해요.
Yangyang wants to go to school.

Vocabulary

음식 food
먹다 eat, have
듣다 listen
읽다 read
가다 go
쓰다 write
쉬다 take a rest
오늘 today
PC방 Internet café

Answers

① 하고 싶어요 ② 무슨

2

A 뭐 먹을래요? What would you like to have?

B 저는 떡볶이하고 김밥을 먹을래요.
I'll have tteokbokki and gimbap.

★ verb + -(으)ㄹ래요

'-(으)ㄹ래요?', '-(으)ㄹ래요.' are used to ask or express the listener's will or intention. When the verb stem ends in any consonant other than 'ㄹ', add '-을래요'. When it ends in a vowel or the consonant 'ㄹ', add '-ㄹ래요'. If a sentence ends in '-(으)ㄹ래요', the subject cannot be in third person.

동사 받침 (O) + -을래요	ㄹ받침, 동사 받침 (X) + -ㄹ래요
먹다 → 먹을래요	가다 → 갈래요
*듣다 → 들을래요	*만들다 → 만들래요

ex A: 양양 씨, 뭐 마실래요? Yangyang, what do you want to drink?
B: 저는 커피를 마실래요. I'd like to have coffee.

★ noun + 하고 + noun

'하고' is used only to connect nouns, especially two nouns, while '그리고' can connect phrases, clauses, and sentences.

ex 마이클은 우유하고 콜라를 사요. Michael buys milk and coke.

Reviews

❶ 뭐 _____요? / 저는 맥주를 _____요.
What do you want to have? / I'd like to have beer.

❷ 뭐 먹을래요? / 라면 _____ 김밥을 먹을래요.
What do you want to have? / I'd like to have ramen and gimbap.

 Tips

In order to connect two or more nouns, you can use '와/과' instead of '하고'. When the last letter has a batchim, '과' is added, but when it ends in a vowel, '와' is added.

ex 교실에 선생님과 학생이 있어요.
There are a teacher and students at classroom.

우유와 콜라 주세요.
I will have milk and coke.

Vocabulary

먹다 eat, have
떡볶이 tteokbokki
김밥 gimbap
듣다 listen
가다 go
만들다 make
마시다 drink
우유 milk
콜라 coke
맥주 beer
라면 ramen

Answers

① 마실래/마실래
② 하고

Key Sentences

3

A 주문하시겠어요? Would you like to order?

B 여기 떡볶이 한 그릇하고 김밥 하나 주세요.
A bowl of tteokbokki and a roll of gimbap, please.

 Tips

When you order something in a restaurant, nouns for materials, liquids, etc. can be countable. For example, you can say '저기요, 갈비탕 하나 주세요' (meaning 'Waiter, a galbitang, please').

★ verb + −(으)세요

'−(으)세요' is used to make a polite request or give a command. When the verb stem ends in any consonant excluding '르', add '−으세요' but when it ends in a vowel, add '−세요'. When the verb stem ends in the consonant 'ㄹ', you should leave it out and add '세요'.

NOTE '−(으)세요' cannot be added to every verb stem.

동사 받침 (O) + −으세요	ㄹ받침, 동사 받침 (X) + −세요
읽다 → 읽으세요	가다 → 가세요

ex 잘 들으세요. Listen carefully.
맛있게 드세요. Enjoy your meal.
안녕히 주무세요. Good night.

★ measurement nouns and counting numbers

When we count numbers, we usually use the native Korean number system. When you count something using a unit of measure, use the following word order: 『noun + number + counting unit』.

ex 공책 두 권하고 지우개 한 개 주세요. Give me two notebooks and an eraser.
저는 한국 친구 스무 명이 있어요. I have twenty Korean friends.

 Vocabulary

주문 order
떡볶이 tteokbokki
그릇 bowl
김밥 gimbap
읽다 read
가다 go
공책 notebook
지우개 eraser
친구 friend
비빔밥 bibimbap

 Reviews

❶ 주문하시겠어요? / 비빔밥 한 _____ 주세요.
Would you like to order? / A bowl of bibimbap, please.

❷ 안녕히 _____. / 안녕히 계세요. Goodbye. / Goodbye.

Answers

① 그릇 ② 가세요.

78

How to Read Numbers

🎧 MP3 07-07

★ **Korean numbers**

Korean numbers are usually used to count numbers.

하나	둘	셋	넷	다섯	여섯	일곱	여덟	아홉	열
1	2	3	4	5	6	7	8	9	10
열하나	열둘	열셋	열넷	열다섯	열여섯	열일곱	열여덟	열아홉	스물
11	12	13	14	15	16	17	18	19	20

But when you count something using a unit of measure, be careful to use the Korean numbers with the following nouns.

개	병	잔(컵)	사람(명)	마리
for things	bottle for juice, water, etc.	cup for juice, coffee, etc.	for persons	for animals
장	그릇	권	시	살
for paper	for food	for book	for time	for age

Numbers change when these nouns are attached.

하나	둘	셋	넷	다섯	여섯	일곱	여덟	아홉	열
→ 한	→ 두	→ 세	→ 네	→ 다섯	→ 여섯	→ 일곱	→ 여덟	→ 아홉	→ 열
열하나	열둘	열셋	열넷	열다섯	열여섯	열일곱	열여덟	열아홉	스물
→ 열한	→ 열두	→ 열세	→ 열네	→ 열다섯	→ 열여섯	→ 열일곱	→ 열여덟	→ 열아홉	→ 스무

ex 공책 두 권하고 지우개 한 개 주세요. Give me two notebooks and an eraser.

저는 한국 친구 스무 명이 있어요. I have twenty Korean friends.

투이 씨, 무슨 음식을 먹고 싶어요?

저는 한국 음식을 먹고 싶어요.

• • •

어서 오세요. 주문하시겠어요?

잠깐만요. 투이 씨, 뭐 먹을래요?

저는 떡볶이를 먹을래요. 동현 씨는요?

저는 김밥을 먹을래요.
저기요. 여기 떡볶이 한 그릇하고 김밥 하나 주세요.

네, 알겠습니다. 잠시만 기다리세요.

• • •

투이 씨, 떡볶이 맛이 어때요?

약간 매워요. 그렇지만 맛있어요.

음식　food	먹다　eat, have	주문　order
떡볶이　tteokbokki	김밥　gimbap	그릇　bowl
잠시만　for a moment	기다리다　wait	맛　taste
맵다　spicy	그렇지만　but	맛있다　delicious

| Donghyun | Thuy, what kind of food do you want to eat? |
| Thuy | I'd like to eat Korean food. |

• • •

Waiter	Welcome. May I take your order?
Donghyun	We need a couple more minutes to decide. Thuy, what would you like to have?
Thuy	I'll have tteokbokki. How about you, Donghyun?
Donghyun	I'll have gimbap.
	Waiter, a bowl of tteokbokki and a roll of gimbap, please.
Waiter	Sure. Wait a moment, please.

• • •

| Donghyun | Thuy, how do you like tteokbokki? |
| Thuy | It's a little spicy but delicious. |

1 Fill in the blanks and say the sentences aloud.

1 뭐 드시겠어요? / 비빔밥 _____ 냉면 주세요.
   What would you like to have? / Bibimbap and naengmyeon, please.

2 뭐 먹을래요? / 라면 한 _____ 주세요.
   What would you like to have? / A bowl of ramen, please.

3 뭐 _____? / 저는 된장찌개를 _____.
   What would you like to have? / I'd like to have doenjang stew.

4 주문하시겠어요? / 커피 _____.
   What would you like to order? / A cup of coffee, please.

2 Match the noun with its counting unit.

책 •   • 장

종이 •   • 명

학생 •   • 권

커피 •   • 잔

라면 •   • 마리

강아지 •   • 그릇

지우개 •   • 개

 Answers 1 1. 하고 2. 그릇 3. 드시겠어요(드실래요)/먹을래요 4. 한 잔 주세요
2 책–권 / 종이–장 / 학생–명 / 커피–잔 / 라면–그릇 / 강아지–마리 / 지우개–개

What Rice Means to the Korean People

Have you ever heard the word 'mukbang'? These days lots of Korean mukbang shows are broadcast all over the world. As the popularity of the shows has soared, the world's interest in Korean food has been increasing. Therefore, many foreigners enjoy favorite Korean foods such as hotdogs, spicy tteokbokki, and spicy pork cutlet.

As you can see from the shows, Korean people think it's very important to have three square meals a day. In the Korean language, '아침', '점심' and '저녁' refer to certain hours of day like morning, afternoon and evening. Also, the three words refer to meals like breakfast, lunch, and dinner respectively. '아침 먹었어요?' literally means 'Did you have breakfast?'. Sometimes the Korean people also use this expression as a kind of greeting like 'Hello' or 'Hi'. Similarly, many Koreans say '언제 같이 밥 먹어요' (meaning 'let's get together for a bite to eat sometime') instead of saying 'Bye'. However, you shouldn't take it seriously because it's just a kind of greeting and a casual remark.

Lesson 08

복습 문제

Review

1 Choose the dialog that sounds natural.

① A: 고맙습니다.　　B: 죄송합니다.

② A: 미안합니다.　　B: 괜찮습니다.

③ A: 다녀왔습니다.　　B: 다녀오겠습니다.

④ A: 실례합니다.　　B: 잘 먹겠습니다.

2 Choose the appropriate word for the blank.

| A | 동현 씨는 학생이에요? |
| B | 아니요, _____이에요. |

① 가수　　② 의사

③ 선생님　　④ 미국 사람

3 Choose the correct answer to the given question.

| A | 미국 사람이에요? |
| B | _____ㅡ. |

① 네, 미국에 가요.

② 네, 베트남 사람이 아니에요.

③ 아니요, 미국에서 왔어요.

④ 아니요, 베트남 사람이에요.

4 Choose the appropriate word for the blank.

| A | 이 사람은 _____예요? |
| B | 제 친구예요. |

① 뭐　　② 어느

③ 어디　　④ 누구

5 Choose the inappropriate word for the blank.

| A | 그건 뭐예요? |
| B | _____ 휴대폰이에요. |

① 제　　② 린다의

③ 저건　　④ 이건

6 Look at the picture and choose the appropriate word for the blank.

> A 식당에 가요?
> B 아니요, _____에 가요.
>
> ① 집   ② 공원
> ③ 학교   ④ 영화관

7 Choose which one is grammatically <u>incorrect</u>.

① 마시다 → 마셔요   ② 만들다 → 만들어요   ③ 운동하다 → 운동해요   ④ 오다 → 오아요

8 Choose which one is grammatically <u>incorrect</u>.

① 예쁘다 → 예뻐요   ② 귀엽다 → 귀여워요   ③ 나쁘다 → 나빠요   ④ 쉽다 → 쉬어요

9 Choose the appropriate word for the blank.

> A 지금 뭐 해요?
> B 도서관_____ 책을 읽어요.
>
> ① 에   ② 도
> ③ 이   ④ 에서

10 Choose the appropriate word for the blank.

> A 투이 씨는 어디에서 친구_____ 만나요?
> B 카페에서 만나요.
>
> ① 이   ② 가
> ③ 을   ④ 를

11 Choose the appropriate response to the given question.

> A 지금 뭐 해요?
> B 음악을 _____.
>
> ① 듣어요   ② 듣아요
> ③ 들어요   ④ 들아요

12 Choose where this conversation would most likely to take place.

> A 뭐 드시겠어요?
> B 돈가스 하나 주세요.

① 식당   ② 공원
③ 카페   ④ 마트

13 Choose the appropriate word for the blank.

> A 동현 씨, 양양 씨가 어디에 있어요?
> B 양양 씨＿＿＿＿ 집에 있어요.

① 은   ② 는
③ 을   ④ 를

14 Choose the appropriate word for the blank.

> A 한국 책이 있어요?
> B 네, 여섯 ＿＿＿＿＿ 있어요.

① 잔   ② 권
③ 살   ④ 명

15 Choose one grammatically correct sentence.

① 사탕 하나 개를 사요.
② 커피 둘 잔이 있어요.
③ 학생 다섯 명이 공부해요.
④ 강아지 넷 마리가 귀여워요.

16 Choose the appropriate word for the blank.

> A 김밥을 먹을래요?
> B 네, 김밥을 ＿＿＿＿＿.

① 먹고 있어요   ② 먹어요
③ 먹고 싶어요   ④ 먹으세요

17 Choose one grammatically correct sentence.

① 저는 도서관에서 공부해요. 그래서 집에 가요.

② 투이 씨는 키가 커요. 그렇지만 키가 작아요.

③ 동현 씨는 공부해요. 그리고 린다 씨도 공부해요.

④ 투이 씨는 베트남 사람이에요. 그래서 학생이에요.

18-19 Look at the picture and choose the best answers.

18

| A | 방에 무엇이 있어요? |
| B | 책상_____ 침대가 있어요. |

① 의   ② 이
③ 가   ④ 하고

19

| A | 고양이가 어디에 있어요? |
| B | 침대 _____에 있어요. |

① 위   ② 아래
③ 앞   ④ 뒤

20 Put the sentences in order in order to make a natural dialog.

① 주문하시겠어요?

② 잠깐만요. 동현 씨, 뭐 먹을래요?

③ 저는 된장찌개를 먹고 싶어요. 투이 씨는요?

④ 저는 김치찌개를 먹을래요.

⑤ 여기요. 된장찌개 하나, 김치찌개 하나 주세요.

① ➡ _____ ➡ _____ ➡ ④ ➡ _____

Lesson 09

어제 뭐 했어요?

What did you do yesterday?

Scan the QR code

Super Easy Korean
for Beginners:
A Self-study Book

Lesson 08

Lesson 09

Video Lectures   Videos for Reviewing

MP3 for Listening   Videos for Words

Lesson 10

Lesson 11

Study Plan

Video Lectures

Book

Videos for Reviewing

Word Lists

Videos for Words

Key Sentences

1

A 동현 씨, 어제 뭐 했어요?
Donghyun, what did you do yesterday?

B 방을 청소하고 좀 쉬었어요.
I cleaned my room and took some rest.

★ verb/adjective + −았/었어요

The past tense verbs and adjectives end in '−았/었어요'. When the vowel before '−다' is 'ㅏ' or 'ㅗ', we add '−았어요'. When the vowel before '−다' is not 'ㅏ' or 'ㅗ', we add '−었어요'. When the base form of a verb ends in '하다' is normally contracted to '−했어요'. Be careful with the words ending in the consonants 'ㅂ' and 'ㄷ' and the vowel 'ㅡ'.

동사/형용사 ㅗ, ㅏ (O) + −았어요	동사/형용사 ㅗ, ㅏ (X) + −었어요	동사/형용사 하다 → −했어요
많다 → 많았어요	맛있다 → 맛있었어요	피곤하다 → 피곤했어요
만나다 → 만났어요	마시다 → 마셨어요	운동하다 → 운동했어요

★ verb/adjective + −고

'그리고' can be used to connect two sentences, while '−고' is used to make two sentences into one.

ex 꽃이 작아요. 그리고 예뻐요. → 꽃이 작고 예뻐요.
The flowers are small and pretty.

저는 어제 영화를 봤어요. 그리고 집에 왔어요. → 저는 어제 영화를 보고 집에 왔어요.
Yesterday I watched a movie and came home.

Reviews

❶ 오늘 뭐 해요? / 책을 _____ 친구를 _____.
What are you doing today? / I'm going to read books and meet my friends.

❷ 책이 어땠어요? / 쉽고 _____.
How was the book? / It was easy and fun.

 Tips

「verb/adjective + 고」 can be used in the past tense as well as the present tense.

NOTE When the verb '일어나다' is connected to another verb, its verb stem '일어나' is combined with '서', not '고'.

ex 아침에 일어나다 + 샤워를 하다 → 아침에 일어나서 샤워를 하다
I woke up in the morning and took a shower.

 Vocabulary

방 room
청소하다 clean
쉬다 take a rest
많다 a lot
만나다 meet
맛있다 delicious
마시다 drink
피곤하다 tired
운동하다 work out
작다 small
예쁘다 pretty
쉽다 easy
재미있다 fun

Answers

① 읽고/만나요   ② 재미있었어요

2

A 투이 씨, 오늘 아침에 뭐 했어요?
Thuy, what did you do this morning?

B 일어나서 세수하고 바로 학교에 왔어요.
I came to school as soon as I got up and washed my face.

★ time + 에

'에' can be used for nouns for measuring time, such as '년' (meaning 'year'), '월' (meaning 'month'), '시' (meaning 'hour'). However, this rule is not always applied.

에 (O)	아침, 점심, 저녁, 낮, 밤, 새벽, 오전, 오후, 작년, 내년 −요일(월/화/수/목/금/토/일), 주말(토요일+일요일) −주(지난주/이번 주/다음 주)
에 (X)	그저께, 어제, 오늘, 내일, 모레, 매일, 지금, 언제, 올해

★ verb + −아/어서

'−아/어서' is used to connect two clauses that have a close relationship. When the vowel before '−다' is 'ㅏ' or 'ㅗ', we add '−아서' to the verb stem. When the vowel before '−다' is not 'ㅏ' or 'ㅗ', we add '−어서'.

동사 ㅗ, ㅏ (O) + −아서	동사 ㅗ, ㅏ (X) + −어서	동사 하다 → 해서
만나다 → 만나서	만들다 → 만들어서	주문하다 → 주문해서
사다 → 사서	씻다 → 씻어서	전화하다 → 전화해서

Reviews

❶ _____ 한국에 왔어요? / 올해 한국에 왔어요.
When did you come to Korea? / I came to Korea this year.

❷ 어제 뭐 했어요? / 친구를 _____ 같이 영화를 봤어요.
What did you do yesterday? / I met my friend and watched a movie together.

 Tips

1. If you need to use more than one adverb of time in a sentence, you should arrange them in order of length of time: the longer units of time come first. And don't forget to only add '에' to the last time noun.

   ex 어제 아침에 뭐 했어요?
   What did you do yesterday morning?

   오늘 오후에 친구를 만나요.
   I'm going to meet my friend this afternoon.

2. '−아/어서' indicates a certain continuity from the first action to the second. On the other hand, '−고' indicates a sequence of the two actions without continuity.

 Vocabulary

세수하다 wash one's face
바로 immediately
씻다 wash

Answers

① 언제 ② 만나서

Key Sentences

3

A 공부 많이 했어요? Did you study a lot?

B 네, 아침부터 지금까지 계속 공부했어요.
Yes, I have been studying since this morning.

★ time + 부터

'부터' (meaning 'from') is used for starting time for an action or event, while '–에' is used for the exact time when something happens.

ex **A:** 언제부터 회사에 가요? From when do you go to work?
B: 내일부터 가요. From tomorrow.
A: 시험 성적이 안 좋아요. I got bad score from test.
B: 그럼 지금부터 열심히 공부하세요. Then study hard from now on.

★ time + 까지

'까지' (meaning 'by' or 'until') is used for the exact time when an action or event stops. The pattern 『시간1 + 부터 + 시간2 + 까지』 represents the duration of an action or event.

ex 다음 주까지 숙제를 하세요.
Do your homework by next week.
지난주부터 오늘까지 야근을 했어요.
I have been working overtime from last week to today.
아침부터 지금까지 계속 공부했어요.
I have been studying from morning until now.

Reviews

❶ 저는 월요일_____ 금요일_____ 학교에 가요.
I go to school from Monday to Friday.

❷ 토요일에 아침_____ 저녁_____ 일이 있어요.
I have appointments from morning to night on Saturday.

Tips

1. '에서' is used after starting point and '까지' describes the destination.

ex 집에서 학교까지 가까워요.
It's near home from school.

2. '부터(에서)', and '까지' are frequently used together, however each can be used on its own.

ex 저는 베트남에서 왔어요.
I'm from Vietnam.

Vocabulary

공부 study
많이 a lot
시험 성적 grade
열심히 hard
숙제를 하다 do one's homework
야근을 하다 work overtime

Answers

① 부터/까지 ② 부터/까지

94

Time

🎧 MP3 09-07

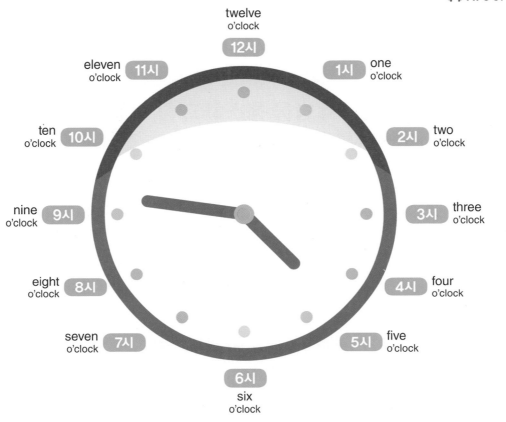

twelve
o'clock
12시

eleven **11시**
o'clock

one **1시**
o'clock

ten **10시**
o'clock

two **2시**
o'clock

nine **9시**
o'clock

three **3시**
o'clock

eight **8시**
o'clock

four **4시**
o'clock

seven **7시**
o'clock

five **5시**
o'clock

6시
six
o'clock

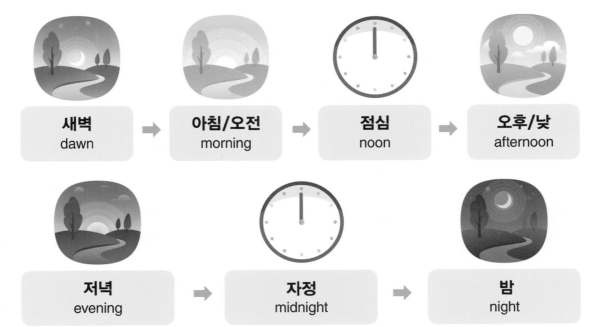

| **새벽** dawn | → | **아침/오전** morning | → | **점심** noon | → | **오후/낮** afternoon |

| **저녁** evening | → | **자정** midnight | → | **밤** night |

🎧 MP3 09-08　🎤 MP3 09-09

 동현 씨, 어제 뭐 했어요?

 아침에 일어나서 방을 청소하고 좀 쉬었어요.
투이 씨는 어제 뭐 했어요?

 도서관에서 한국어를 공부했어요.

 그래요? 공부 많이 했어요?

 그럼요, 아침부터 저녁까지 했어요.

 와, 정말요? 도서관에 혼자 갔어요?

 아니요, 친구를 만나서 같이 갔어요.
너무 피곤했어요. 그래서 오늘 늦게 일어났어요.

 그렇군요. 오늘 학교에 늦었어요?

 아니요. 일어나서 세수하고 바로 학교에 왔어요.

어제 yesterday	일어나다 get up	청소하다 clean
쉬다 take a rest	공부하다 study	많이 a lot
혼자 alone	친구 friend	만나다 meet
피곤하다 tired	늦게 late	
세수하다 wash one's face	바로 immediately	

Thuy	Donghyun, what did you do yesterday?
Donghyun	I cleaned my room as soon as I woke up, and then I took some rest.
	What did you do yesterday, Thuy?
Thuy	I studied Korean.
Donghyun	Did you? Did you study a lot?
Thuy	Sure. I studied from morning to night.
Donghyun	Wow, really? Did you go to the library alone?
Thuy	No, I went there with my friend.
	I felt tired, so I got up late this morning.
Donghyun	I understand. Were you late for school today?
Thuy	Fortunately no. I came to school as soon as I woke up and washed my face.

1 **Unscramble the words and read the dialog aloud.**

1 A **어제 뭐 했어요?** What did you do yesterday?

 B _____. [카페/커피/가서/마셨어요/를/에]
 I went to the café and drank coffee.

2 A **어제 투이 씨를 만났어요?** Did you meet Thuy yesterday?

 B **네,** _____. [투이 씨/만나서/를/커피/마셨어요/를]
 Yes, I met Thuy and drank coffee with her.

2 **Write the proper word in each pair of parentheses.**

1 A **오늘 뭐 해요?** What are you doing today?

 B **학교에 _____ 한국어 공부를 해요.** [가다] I go to school and study Korean.

2 A **어제 뭐 했어요?** What did you do yesterday?

 B **집에서 _____ 쉬었어요.** [청소를 하다]
 I cleaned the house and took a rest.

3 A **언제 _____ 한국어를 공부했어요?** Since when did you start studying Korean?

 B **지난달 _____ 한국어를 공부했어요.** I started studying Korean from last month.

Downtown Seoul

Myeongdong

Myeongdong is the most popular place for foreign tourists. You can shop at major department stores, stay at a fancy hotel and eat at a nice restaurant. In addition, you can enjoy different street foods from around the world. The public transportation is convenient around this area. Therefore, it's easy to go to other tourist attractions, such as Jongno, Dongdaemun Market, and Namsan Seoul Tower.

Insadong and Samcheongdong

The area around Insadong and Samcheongdong is very popular for foreigners, too. You can try on hanbok (traditional Korean clothes) and enjoy traditional Korean tea here. You can also buy special souvenirs for your family and friends.

Dongdaemun

Dongdaemun is a shopping district filled with lots of shopping malls as well as traditional markets. A night market is held here every night and you can enjoy different kinds of food. Come and enjoy!

Hongik University

The area around Hongik University is a hot spot among young people. This is a good place for shopping and dining. The streets are lined with nice cafés and restaurants as well as different kinds of shops that sell clothes, accessories and cosmetics. The best way to get there from Incheon International Airport is taking the Airport Railroad Express (AREX).

Itaewon

Itaewon is a unique multicultural district of Seoul that has many restaurants, pubs, souvenir shops, and clubs. You can enjoy different foods from around the world in fancy restaurants.

Lesson 10

생일이 언제예요?

When is your birthday?

Key Sentences

1

A 투이 씨, 마리아 씨의 생일이 언제예요?
Thuy, when is Maria's birthday?

B 6월 25일이에요. It's June 25th.

★ numbers (Sino–Korean numbers)

When we count numbers, we usually say 하나, 둘, 셋, 넷, etc.
However, when we talk about days, time, prices, phone numbers,
floor numbers and house numbers, we use the Sino–Korean
number system: 일, 이, 삼, 사, etc.

1	2	3	4	5	6	7	8	9	10	100	1000	10000
일	이	삼	사	오	육	칠	팔	구	십	백	천	만

★ time (1) – days and weeks

월	일, 이, 삼, 사, 오, 육[유월], 칠, 팔, 구, 십[시월], 십일, 십이
일	일, 이, 삼, 사, 오, 육, 칠, 팔, 구, 십, 십일, 십이, 십삼, 십사, 십오, 십육[심뉵], 십칠, 십팔, 십구, 이십, 이십일, 이십이, 이십삼, 이십사, 이십오, 이십육[이심뉵], 이십칠, 이십팔, 이십구, 삼십, 삼십일
요일	월요일, 화요일, 수요일, 목요일, 금요일, 토요일, 일요일

ex A: 오늘이 몇 월 며칠이에요?/언제예요?　What date is it today?

B: 10월 16일이에요.　It's October 16th.

A: 오늘이 무슨 요일이에요?　What day is it today?

B: 금요일이에요.　It's Friday.

Reviews

❶ A 크리스마스가 _____월_____이에요?
What date is Christmas day?

❷ B _____이에요/예요.　It's December 25th.

Tips

How do you say 1,000,000 in
Korean? Principally, we should
say '일백만', but we usually say
'백만', dropping '일' before '백만'.

Vocabulary

크리스마스　Christmas

Answers

① 몇/며칠　② 12월 25일

2

A 투이 씨, 안으로 들어오세요. Come in, Thuy.

B 네, 고마워요. 양양 씨는 아직 안 왔어요?
Thank you. Isn't Yangyang here yet?

⭐ 안 + verb/adjectives

To make a statement negative, add '안' before the verb or adjective:
the negative form of the verb '하다' is '안 하다'. However, you should
be careful when you add '안' to adjectives that end in '하다'.

NOTE The negative form of the verb '있다' is '없다', not '안 있다'.

ex 마이클은 오늘 학교에 안 가요. Michael doesn't go to school today.
린다는 운동(을) 안 해요. Linda doesn't work out.

⭐ place + (으)로 가다/오다

'(으)로' is used to indicate direction. Nouns related to locations and
directions and place names come before '(으)로 가다/오다'. When
the last letter of the noun ends in a consonant, we add '으로' to the
noun. When it ends in a vowel, we add '로'.

명사 받침(O) + 으로	명사 받침ㄹ, 받침(X) + 로
밖 → 밖으로	위 → 위로

ex **A:** 어디로 가요? Where should I go?
B: 교실로 오세요. Come to the classroom.

Reviews

❶ 운동했어요? / 아니요, _____.
Did you work out? / No, I didn't work out.

❷ 5층_____ 올라오세요.
Come up to the fifth floor.

Vocabulary

들어오다 enter, come in
들어가다 enter, come in
나오다 come out
나가다 get out
올라오다 come up
올라가다 go up
내려오다 come down
내려가다 go down
층 floor

Answers

① 운동 안 했어요 ② 으로

Key Sentences

🎧 MP3 10-05 🎤 MP3 10-06

3

A 동현 씨, 지금 몇 시예요? Donghyun, what time is it?

B 7시 30분이에요. It's 7:30.

★ time (2) – hours & minutes

You've learned about the 『time + 에』 form. What should you say if there are two or more time expressions: '12월 25일, 9:00', and '친구를 만나요?'. We say '12월 25일 9시에 친구를 만나요' (meaning 'We'll meet at 9:00, the 25th of December'), adding '에' to the last time expression.

시	한, 두, 세, 네, 다섯, 여섯, 일곱, 여덟, 아홉, 열, 열한, 열두
분	일, 이, 삼, 사, 오, 육, 칠, 팔, 구, 십, 십오 ... 삼십(= 반)

ex **A:** 몇 시예요? What time is it now?
B: 12시 30분이에요(= 반이에요). 12:30.

★ 몇

When we ask about certain numbers or how many there are of something, we use '몇'.

ex **A:** 가족이 몇 명이에요? How many people are in your family?
B: 네 명이에요. There are four.
A: 전화번호가 몇 번이에요? What is your phone number?
B: 010–1234–5678이에요. It's 010-1234-5678.
A: 사무실은 몇 층에 있어요? What floor is the office on?
B: 5층에 있어요. It's on the fifth floor.

Reviews

❶ _____시예요? / 12시예요. What time is it? / It's 12 o'clock.

❷ 언제 영화를 봐요? / 오늘 오후 _____에 봐요.
When are you watching the movie? / I'm watching the movie at 6:00 pm today.

 Tips

We say each digit of a telephone number separately, pausing at the first hyphen and saying '에' at the second hyphen. The figure 0 is usually called '공' (gong).

 Vocabulary

지금 now
시 hour
분 minute
30분 half-hour
가족 family
전화번호 phone number
사무실 office
층 floor

Answers
① 몇 ② 여섯 시

104

Date

월요일
Monday

화요일
Tuesday

수요일
Wednesday

목요일
Thursday

금요일
Friday

토요일
Saturday

일요일
Sunday

1월
January

2월
February

3월
March

4월
April

5월
May

6월
June

7월
July

8월
August

9월
September

10월
October

11월
November

12월
December

오늘
today

내일
tomorrow

어제
yesterday

그저께
the day before yesterday

모레
the day after tomorrow

주말
weekend

지난주
last week

이번 주
this week

다음 주
next week

작년
last year

올해
this year

내년
next year

Dialog

🎧 MP3 10-08　🎙 MP3 10-09

 다음 주 토요일 6시에 양양 씨의 생일 파티가 있어요.
투이 씨도 오세요.

 네, 좋아요. 파티는 어디에서 해요?

 마리아 씨 집 근처 식당에서 해요.

 네, 알겠어요.

 참, 투이 씨, 마리아 씨 전화번호가 몇 번이에요?
양양 씨가 마리아 씨도 초대하고 싶어 해요.

 잠깐만요. 010-1234-5678이에요.

 고마워요.

· · ·

 투이 씨, 왔어요? 2층으로 올라가세요.

 네, 알겠어요. 마리아 씨도 왔어요?

 아니요, 마리아 씨는 아직 안 왔어요.

생일 파티 birthday party	참 Oh	초대하다 invite
잠깐만요. Wait a minute.	아직 yet	

106

Donghyun	Yangyang's birthday party is at 6 o'clock next Saturday.
	Can you join us, Thuy?
Thuy	Sure. Where is the party?
Donghyun	A restaurant near Maria's.
Thuy	All right.
Donghyun	Oh, Thuy, do you remember what Maria's phone number is?
	Yangyang wants to invite Maria, too.
Thuy	Wait a minute. It's 010-1234-5678.
Donghyun	Thank you.

• • •

Donghyun	Oh, you are here. Go upstairs.
Thuy	Okay. Is Maria here?
Donghyun	No, she is not here yet.

Exercises

1 Unscramble the words and read the dialog aloud.

1 _____. [저/오늘/공부/는/안/했어요]
I didn't study today.

2 _____? [이/생일/며칠/월/몇/이에요]
When is your birthday?

3 _____. [이에요/지금/은/오전/아홉 시/삼십 분]
It is nine thirty am.

2 Choose the proper word for the blank.

청첩장	Wedding Invitation
사랑하는 두 사람이 만났습니다. 꼭 참석하셔서 축하해 주십시오.	The two people who love each other are getting together. Join us and bless us.
2020년 6월 6일 토요일 오후 6:30 〈사랑예식장〉 강남역 도보 10분	At 6:00 pm Saturday the sixth of June, 2020 〈Sarang Wedding Hall〉 a 10-minute walk from Gangnam Station

1 **결혼식이 언제예요?** When is the wedding?

  → _____월_____일이에요. It's June 6th.

2 **결혼식이 몇 시에 시작해요?** What time does the wedding start?

  → _____ 이요. It starts at 6:30.

Korean National Holidays

In Korea, Seollal is one of the major holidays. It is observed on the first day of the Korean lunar calendar. On New Year's day, people wear new clothes called seolbim. Before having breakfast, they visit ancestral graves (seongmyo) and take a deep bow to their elders (sebae) in order to pay respect. And then the whole family

gets together and eats rice soup (tteokguk) and dumplings (mandu). When you eat tteokguk on New Year's morning, it means you are now a year older.

Chuseok, which is celebrated on the 15th day of August on the Lunar calendar, is one of Korea's most important holidays. On Chuseok, Koreans give thanks to their ancestors for a full harvest. They visit their ancestral graves and perform memorial services. They make rice cakes (songpyeon), and it is believed that the women who make beautiful songpyeon will have a beautiful babies.

Lesson 11

같이 명동에 갈까요?

Shall we go to Myeongdong?

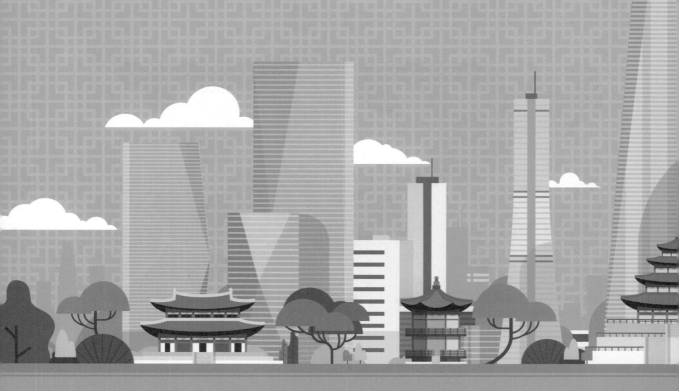

Key Sentences

1

A 투이 씨, 주말에 시간이 있어요?
Thuy, do you have time this weekend?

B 토요일에는 바쁘지만 일요일에는 괜찮아요.
I'm busy on Saturday but free on Sunday.

★ verb/adjective ＋ –지만

When we connect contrasting phrases or clauses, we add '–지만' to the verb or adjective stems.

동사/형용사 받침 (O/X) ＋ –지만	
가다 → 가지만	먹다 → 먹지만
예쁘다 → 예쁘지만	맵다 → 맵지만

ex 린다 씨는 키가 커요. 그렇지만 저는 키가 작아요.
→ 린다 씨는 키가 크지만 저는 키가 작아요. Linda is tall, but I'm short.

★ noun ＋ 은/는 (3)

'은/는' is mainly used in three different ways: identifying a topic, contrasting or comparing, and referring to what you mentioned before.

ex 양양은 자전거가 있어요. 그렇지만 저는 자전거가 없어요.
Yangyang has a bicycle. But I don't have a bike.

Reviews

① 이 옷은 아주 _____ 너무 비싸요. [예쁘다]
This clothes is very pretty, but too expensive.

② 마이클 씨는 학생이지만 양양 씨_____ 회사원이에요.
Michael is a student, but Yangyang is an office worker.

 Tips

1. In the past tense sentences, '–지만' changes to '–았/었/했지만' depending on how the stem word ends.
   ex 가다 → 갔지만
   마시다 → 마셨지만
   조용하다 → 조용했지만

2. '–은/는' can normally be added to most nouns. If a noun is a place name, we add '–에서는'. If a noun is related to time, we add '–에는'.
   ex 토요일에는 쉬었어요. 그렇지만 일요일에는 일했어요.
   I rested on Saturday. But I worked on Sunday.

 Vocabulary

주말 weekend
바쁘다 busy
그렇지만 but
키가 크다 tall
키가 작다 short
자전거 bike
옷 clothes
비싸다 expensive

Answers

① 예쁘지만 ② 는

112

2

A 오후에 같이 명동에 갈까요?
Why don't we go to Myeongdong this afternoon?

B 미안해요. 일이 있어서 안 돼요. I'm sorry. I have another plan.

⭐ (우리) (같이) verb + −(으)ㄹ까요?

'−(으)ㄹ까요?' is used to make a suggestion. When the verb or adjective stem ends in a vowel or the consonant 'ㄹ', we add '−ㄹ까요?'. When the stem ends in any consonant other than 'ㄹ', we add '−을까요?'.

동사 받침 (O) + −을까요?	동사 ㄹ받침, 받침 (X) + −ㄹ까요?
먹다 → 먹을까요?	가다 → 갈까요?

 우리 같이 밥을 먹을까요? Should we eat together?
같이 도서관에서 공부할까요? Should we study at our library together?

⭐ verb/adjective + −아/어서 (reason)

'−아/어/해서' is used when we connect clauses of cause and result. When the last vowel in stem word before '−다' is 'ㅏ' or 'ㅗ', we add '−아서'. When the vowel before '−다' is not 'ㅏ' or 'ㅗ', we add '−어서'. When the sentence ends in '하다', we use '해서'.

동사/형용사 ㅗ, ㅏ (O) + −아서	동사/형용사 ㅗ, ㅏ (X) + −어서	동사/형용사 하다 → 해서
가다 → 가서	재미있다 → 재미있어서	운동하다 → 운동해서

 머리가 아파요. 그래서 병원에 가요 → 머리가 아파서 병원에 가요.
I go to the hospital because I have a headache.

 Reviews

❶ 날씨가 좋아요. 그래서 기분이 좋아요. → _____.
I feel good because the weather is good.

❷ 마이클 씨는 학생_____ 매일 학교에 가요.
Michael is a student, so he goes to school every day.

Tips

If the word is a noun, we say 『명사 + (이)라서』 or 『명사 + 이어서/여서』. When the noun ends in a consonant, we add '이라서/이어서' to the noun. When the noun ends in a vowel, we add '라서/여서'.

Vocabulary

오후 afternoon
머리가 아프다 have a headache
병원 hospital
기분이 좋다 feel good

Answers

① 날씨가 좋아서 기분이 좋아요
② 이라서(이어서)

🎧 **MP3** 11-05　🎤 **MP3** 11-06

3

A 명동역 어때요? What about Myeongdong Station?

B 네, 그럼 (우리) 명동역에서 두 시에 만나요.
Sounds good. Then, let's meet at Myeongdong Station at 2 o'clock.

⭐ **time/place + 이/가(은/는) 어때요?**

This expression is used to arrange when or where to meet someone. When the noun ends in a consonant, we add '이(은) 어때요?' to the noun. When the noun ends in a vowel, we add '가(는) 어때요?'.

ex 명동역(이) 어때요? How about Myeongdong Station?
　　두 시(가) 어때요? How about two o'clock?
　　이건 어때요? How about this?

⭐ **(우리) (같이) verb + ―아/어요**

『(우리) (같이) verb + ―아/어요』 is used as the answer to the question 『verb + ―(으)ㄹ까요?』. This pattern can be also used to make a suggestion.

동사 ㅗ, ㅏ (O) + ―아요	동사 ㅗ, ㅏ (X) + ―어요	동사 하다 → 해요
가다 → 가요	먹다 → 먹어요	운동하다 → 운동해요
놀다 → 놀아요	*듣다 → 들어요	공부하다 → 공부해요

ex (우리) 좀 쉬어요. Let's have some rest.
　　(우리) 같이 노래를 들어요. Let's listen to the song together.

 Reviews

❶ 우리 같이 쇼핑할까요? = 우리 같이 _____.
　 Should we shop together?

❷ 뭘 먹을까요? / _____? [비빔밥]
　 What do you want to eat? / How about bibimbap?

 Tips

When you make a suggestion, you cannot say 『noun + 은/는 ― 아/어요』. '―은/는' is only used as the subject of a declarative sentence.

ex Let's play together. (✓) (suggestion)
　　We play together. (✓) (the present tense)

📓 **Vocabulary**

명동역 Myeongdong Station
만나다 meet
쉬다 have a rest
듣다 listen
비빔밥 bibimbap

Answers

① 쇼핑해요　② 비빔밥 어때요?

Expressions about Appointments

-와/과 약속을 하다
make an appointment with somebody

-와/과 약속이 있다
have an appointment with somebody

약속이 없다
have no appointment

약속 장소를 정하다/잡다
arrange / book an appointment

약속 시간을 정하다/잡다
arrange a date and time

약속을 거절하다
cancel an appointment

시간이 없다
have no time

시간이 있다
have time

일이 생기다
have an urgent matter (to deal with)

일이 있다
have work to do

일이 많다
have a lot of work to do

바쁘다
be busy

Dialog

🎧 MP3 11-08 🎤 MP3 11-09

 투이 씨, 이번 주말에 시간이 있어요?
같이 쇼핑할까요?

 미안해요. 이번 주는 약속이 있어서 안 돼요.

 그래요? 그럼 다음 주 월요일은 어때요?

 오전에는 수업이 있지만 오후에는 괜찮아요.
월요일에 만날까요?

 좋아요. 몇 시에 만날까요?

 오후 2시가 어때요?

 네, 좋아요.

 어디에서 만날까요?

 명동역 4번 출구 어때요?

 좋아요. 그럼 다음 주 월요일 오후 2시에
명동역 4번 출구에서 만나요.

주말 weekend	시간이 있다 have time	다음 주 next week
오전 morning	오후 afternoon	괜찮다 okay, fine
명동역 Myeongdong Station	출구 exit	

Donghyun	Thuy, do you have time this weekend? Why don't we go shopping?
Thuy	I'm sorry, I can't. I have an appointment this week.
Donghyun	Do you? How about next Monday?
Thuy	I have go to classes in the morning, but I'm free in the afternoon. Can we make it on Monday?
Donghyun	Sure. What time shall we meet?
Thuy	How about two?
Donghyun	Sounds good.
Thuy	Where shall we meet?
Donghyun	How about Myeongdong Station Exit 4?
Thuy	Okay, Let's say at 2:00 next Monday, at Myeongdong Station Exit 4.

1 Fill in the blanks and say the sentences aloud.

1 저는 외국 사람이에요. 그렇지만 한국에서 살아요.

   → 저는 외국 사람_____ 한국에서 살아요.
   I'm a foreigner, but I live in Korea.

2 저 가게는 음식이 아주 맛있어요. 그렇지만 좀 비싸요.

   → 저 가게는 음식이 아주 _____ 좀 비싸요.
   The food at that restaurant is delicious, but it's a little expensive.

2 Fill in the blanks of the dialog.

A 투이 씨, 주말에 시간이 있어요? 같이 영화를 볼까요?
   Thuy, do you have time this weekend? Why don't we go to the theater?

B 네, 좋아요. 1_____ 만날까요?
   Sounds good. What time shall we meet?

A 일요일 세 시가 어때요?
   How about 3 o'clock this Sunday?

B 네, 좋아요. 2_____ 에서 만날까요?
   Fine with me. Where should we meet?

A 명동역에서 3_____ .
   Let's meet at Myeongdong Station.

B 좋아요. 그럼 일요일에 명동역에서 봐요.
   Good. Then see you on Sunday at Myeongdong Station.

Answers **1** 1. 이지만 2. 맛있지만
         2 1. 언제 2. 어디 3. 만나요

Meaning of "Let's get together for a bite to eat sometime."

When Korean people come across someone they know, they often say '우리 나중에 같이 밥 먹어요' (meaning 'let's get together for a bite to eat sometime') or '나중에 같이 술 한 잔 해요' (meaning 'let's have a drink sometime'). But you don't have to take it so seriously. They say it as a kind of greeting, and it has no special meaning. So don't wait for them to invite you for a drink or a meal.

Lesson 12

내일은 아마
더울 거예요.

It's probably going to be hot
tomorrow.

Key Sentences

🎧 MP3 12-01 🎤 MP3 12-02

1

A 베트남은 요즘 더워요?
Is it hot in Vietnam these days?

B 네, 아주 덥고 비가 자주 내려요.
Yes, it's very hot and often rains.

★ seasonal / weather vocabulary

계절	봄	여름	가을	겨울
날씨	따뜻하다	덥다 비가 오다/내리다	시원하다 바람이 불다	춥다 눈이 오다/내리다

★ adverbs of frequency

An adverb of frequency describes how often an action happens.
It is located in front of a verb.

매일	자주	가끔	거의 안	전혀 안
every day	**often**	**sometimes**	**rarely**	**never**

ex 나는 매일 운동해요. I exercise every day.
저는 자주 운동해요. I exercise often.
저는 가끔 운동해요. I exercise sometimes.
저는 운동을 거의 안 해요. I rarely exercise.
저는 운동을 전혀 안 해요. I never exercise.

 Reviews

❶ 베트남에 눈이 자주 와요? / 아니요. 전혀 _____ 와요.
Does it snow often in Vietnam? / No, not at all.

❷ 마이클 씨는 무슨 계절을 좋아해요? / 날씨가 시원해서 _____이 좋아요.
Michael, which season do you like? / I like autumn because it's cool.

 Tips

1. To some 'often' means very frequently, to others sometimes or once in a blue moon.

2. Check where the adverbs '거의 안' (meaning 'barely') and '전혀 안' (meaning 'never') are placed in a sentence.

 Vocabulary

요즘 these days
덥다 hot
비가 오다/내리다 rain
날씨 weather
따뜻하다 warm
시원하다 cool
바람이 불다 windy
춥다 cold
눈이 오다/내리다 snow

Answers

① 안
② 가을

2

A 동현 씨는 무슨 계절을 좋아해요?
What season do you like, Donghyun?

B 날씨가 춥지 않아서 봄을 좋아해요.
I like spring because it is getting warmer.

★ verb/adjective + −지 않다

Like 『안 +verb/adjective』, the pattern 『verb/adjective + −지 않다』 makes a statement negative. Usually 『안 + verb/adjective』 is used in speech, while '−지 않다' is used both in speech and in writing.

> **ex** 오늘은 공부 안 할 거예요. = 오늘은 공부하지 않을 거예요.
> I will not study today.
> 어제는 안 더웠어요. = 어제는 덥지 않았어요.
> It wasn't hot yesterday.

★ adjective + −아/어하다 → verb

One of the common mistakes Korean learners make is to confuse '좋다' with '좋아하다'. In short, '좋다' is an adjective and '좋아하다' is a verb. Usually a subject ending in '이/가' comes before an adjective, while an object ending in '을/를' comes before a verb.

> **ex** 저는 비빔밥을 좋아하고, 마이클 씨는 김치찌개를 좋아해요.
> I like bibimbap, and Michael likes kimchi stew.
> 저는 여름이 싫어요. (= 저는 여름을 싫어해요.) I don't like summer.

 Tips

『Verb+ −고 싶다』 is used like adjective, so if you want to express third person's desire, you must use 『verb+ −고 싶어 하다』.

 Vocabulary

김치찌개 kimchi stew
여름 summer

 Reviews

❶ 양양 씨는 운동을 좋아해요? / 아니요. 저는 운동을 _____.
Yangyang, do you like exercise? / No. I don't like exercise.

❷ 저는 커피를 마시고 싶어요. 그렇지만 마이클은 커피를 안 _____.
I want to drink coffee. But Michael doesn't want to drink coffee.

 Answers

① 좋아하지 않아요
② 마시고 싶어 해요

🎧 **MP3** 12-05 🎤 **MP3** 12-06

3

A 내일은 날씨가 어떨까요?
What is the weather going to be like tomorrow?

B 아주 더울 거예요. It's going to be very hot.

★ verb/adjective + ㅡ(으)ㄹ 거예요 (1)

'ㅡ(으)ㄹ 거예요' is used to express expectations for a future event or state. When the verb or adjective stem ends in a consonant, we add '을 거예요'. When the stem ends in a vowel or the consonant 'ㄹ', we add 'ㅡㄹ 거예요'.

동사/형용사 받침(O) + ㅡ을 거예요	동사/형용사 ㄹ, 받침(X) + ㅡㄹ 거예요
먹다 → 먹을 거예요	가다 → 갈 거예요

ex (아마) 날씨가 더울 거예요. (Probably) the weather will be hot.

마이클 씨 여자 친구는 예쁠 거예요. Michael's girlfriend would be pretty.

★ verb/adjective + ㅡ(으)ㄹ까요?

'ㅡ(으)ㄹ까요?' can be used when we're wondering what a third person is thinking. This expression cannot have a subject in first or second person.

동사/형용사 받침(O) + ㅡ을까요?	동사/형용사 ㄹ, 받침(X) + ㅡㄹ까요?
재미있다 → 재미있을까요?	가다 → 갈까요?

ex 내일은 날씨가 맑을까요? Is it sunny tomorrow?

이 음식은 맛있을까요? Is this food delicious?

Reviews

❶ 마이클 씨는 지금 뭐 _____? / 아마 공부할 거예요.
I wonder what Michael is doing now. / He is probably studying.

❷ 이 식당, 음식이 맛있을까요? / 아마 _____.
Do you think this restaurant serves good food? / Maybe it's good.

 Tips

1. The base form of '어때요' is '어떻다'. The consonant 'ㅎ' in '어떻다' is dropped when 'ㅡ(으)나' or 'ㅡ아/어' is added to the stem. For example, when '어요' is added to the stem, '어떻다' is changed to '어때요'. When 'ㅡ았/었어요' is added, it is changed to '어땠어요'. When 'ㅡ(으)ㄹ까요?' is added, it is changed to '어떨까요?'.

2. 'ㅡ았/었을 거예요' is used when we are speculating about past events.

ex A 투이 씨는 어디에 갔어요?
Where did Thuy go?

B 글쎄요. (아마) 집에 갔을 거예요.
I don't know. (Maybe) she went home.

 Vocabulary

내일 tomorrow
날씨 weather
덥다 hot
여자 친구 girlfriend
맑다 sunny, clear
음식 food
맛있다 delicious
공부하다 study

Answers

① 할까요 ② 맛있을 거예요

'ㅂ' Irregular Conjugation

When some adjective or verb stems ending in the final consonant 'ㅂ' are followed by a vowel, 'ㅂ' changes into '우' (some of them changes '오') dropping 'ㅂ'. However, not every verb and adjective whose stem ends in 'ㅂ' is irregular. For example, when the verb '입다' (meaning 'wear') is combined with '-어요', 'ㅂ' is not dropped. It is changed to '입어요'.

기본형(사전형)	-아/어요	-았/었어요
덥다	더워요	더웠어요
춥다	추워요	추웠어요
어렵다	어려워요	어려웠어요
쉽다	쉬워요	쉬웠어요
맵다	매워요	매웠어요
*눕다(동사)	누워요	누웠어요
*돕다(동사)	도와요	도왔어요
입다	입어요	입었어요

기본형(사전형)	-(으)ㄹ 거예요	-고
덥다	더울 거예요	덥고
춥다	추울 거예요	춥고
어렵다	어려울 거예요	어렵고
쉽다	쉬울 거예요	쉽고
맵다	매울 거예요	맵고
*눕다(동사)	누울 거예요	눕고
*돕다(동사)	도울 거예요	돕고
입다	입을 거예요	입고

Dialog

🎧 MP3 12-07 🎤 MP3 12-08

 투이 씨는 무슨 계절을 좋아해요?

 저는 봄을 좋아해요. 날씨가 춥지 않고 따뜻해서 좋아요.

 저도 꽃이 많이 피어서 봄이 좋아요.
그런데 투이 씨, 요즘 베트남은 날씨가 어때요?

 아주 더워요. 그리고 비가 자주 내려요.

 그래요? 한국도 여름에는 덥고 비가 자주 와요.

 그럼, 내일은 날씨가 어떨까요?

 지금은 장마철이라서 아마 내일도 비가 올 거예요.

 그렇군요.

 네, 우산이 필요할 거예요. 우산 꼭 챙기세요.

계절 season	봄 spring	날씨 weather
춥다 cold	따뜻하다 warm	꽃 flower
피다 bloom	덥다 hot	비가 오다 rain
내일 tomorrow	장마철 the rainy season	필요하다 need
우산 umbrella	챙기다 take	

Donghyun	Which season do you like, Thuy?
Thuy	I like spring because it's warm.
Donghyun	I also like spring because there are flowers everywhere. Thuy, what is the weather like in Vietnam these days?
Thuy	It's very hot and often rains.
Donghyun	Is it? Korea has hot, rainy summers.
Thuy	Then, how will the weather be tomorrow?
Donghyun	It's the rainy season these days, so it'll probably rain again tomorrow.
Thuy	I see.
Donghyun	You'll need an umbrella tomorrow. Take one with you.

1 **Fill in the blanks and say the sentences aloud.**

한국에는 사계절이 있어요.

_____은 따뜻해요. 꽃이 많이 피어서 아주 예뻐요.

_____은 더워요. 그리고 비가 많이 와요. 우산이 필요해요.

_____은 시원해요. 산에 단풍이 들어서 사람들이 소풍을 많이 가요.

_____은 아주 춥고 눈이 많이 와요.

Korea has four seasons. It is warm in the spring. At this time, Korea is beautiful because there are flowers everywhere. In the summer it is hot and rains a lot. You need an umbrella. It is cool in the autumn. Leaves turn red or yellow. People go hiking in the mountains to enjoy colorful trees. In the winter, it is very cold and snows a lot.

2 **Fill in the blanks.**

1 A 동현 씨, 투이 씨는 어디에 있어요? Donghyun, where is Thuy?

   B 글쎄요. 아마 집에 _____. Well... she's probably at home.

2 A 저 식당은 음식이 _____? Do you think that restaurant serves good food?

   B 저 가게는 사람이 많아요. 아마 맛있을 거예요.
      There are lots of people in there. I think it's good.

3 A 투이 씨는 어느 계절을 _____? Which season do you like, Thuy?

   B 저는 봄이 _____. I like spring.

128

Why Is It 'Cool' When It Is Hot?

You may have heard Korean people say '시원하다' (meaning 'it's cool') while they're eating hot food. It may sound strange to you, but there is a saying '이열치열' (meaning 'fight fire with fire'). It means that you can beat the heat by eating hot food. If you sweat a lot when you eat hot food, you'll feel coolness like a gust of wind. That's why Korean people say '시원하다' eating hot food.

Lesson 13

한정식을 먹으러 갈 거예요.

I'll go for a traditional Korean
table d'hôte (hanjeongsik).

Key Sentences

1

A 주말에 뭐 할 거예요? What are you going to do this weekend?

B 한정식을 먹으러 인사동에 갈 거예요.
I'll go to Insadong for a traditional Korean table d'hôte.

⭐ verb + -(으)ㄹ 거예요 (2)

'-(으)ㄹ 거예요' is used to express future confirmed plans or intentions. When the verb stem ends in any consonant excluding '르', '-을 거예요' is added. When the verb stem ends in the consonant '르' or a vowel, '-ㄹ 거예요' is added.

동사 받침 (O) + -을 거예요	동사 ㄹ, 받침 (X) + -ㄹ 거예요
먹다 → 먹을 거예요	보다 → 볼 거예요

ex 내일 마이클과 밥을 먹을 거예요. I will eat with Michael tomorrow.
다음 주부터 공부할 거예요. I will study from next week.

⭐ verb + -(으)러 가다/오다/다니다

『Verb + -(으)러 가다/오다/다니다』 is usually used to express purpose. When the verb stem ends in any consonant excluding '르', we add '-으러 가다'. When the verb stem ends in the consonant '르' or a vowel, we add '-러 가다'.

동사 받침 (O) + -으러 가다	동사 ㄹ, 받침 (X) + -러 가다
먹다 → 먹으러 가다	보다 → 보러 가다

ex 편지를 보내러 우체국에 가요. I go to the post office to send a letter.

Reviews

❶ 오늘 뭐 할 거예요? / 도서관에서 친구를 _____.
What are you going to do today? / I'm meeting my friend at the library.

❷ 왜 한국에 왔어요? / 한국어를 _____ 왔어요.
Why did you come to Korea? / I came to study Korean.

👜 **Tips**

If you want to talk about the place, you can say either 『place + 에 -(으)러 가다』 or 『-(으)러 + place + 에 가다』 form. You cannot say '가다' and '오다' at the same time, such as '가러 오다' or '오러 가다'.

📓 **Vocabulary**

주말 weekend
한정식 traditional Korean table d'hôte
인사동 Insadong
다음 주 next week
편지 letter
보내다 send
우체국 post office
도서관 library
공부하다 study

Answers

① 만날 거예요 ② 공부하러

132

❷

A 투이 씨는 한정식을 먹어 봤어요?

Thuy, have you ever had a traditional Korean table d'hôte?

B 아니요. 아직 안 먹어 봤어요. Not yet.

★ verb + −아/어 보다 (1) (−아/어 봤어요)

『Verb + −아/어 보다』 is used to talk about an attempt to have a special experience. When the verb stem ends in the vowel 'ㅏ' or 'ㅗ', we add '−아 보다'. When the verb stem doesn't end in the vowel 'ㅏ' or 'ㅗ', we add '−어 보다'. When the verb stem ends in '−하다', we use '해 보다'. Note that this expression is not used when you talk about your daily routine. Accordingly, '저는 매일 학교에 가 봤어요' (meaning 'I have been to school every day') sounds awkward.

동사 ㅗ, ㅏ (O) + −아 보다	동사 ㅗ, ㅏ (X) + −어 보다	하다 → 해 보다
가다 → 가 보다	마시다 → 마셔 보다	운동하다 → 운동해 보다
보다 → 봐 보다(×)	먹다 → 먹어 보다	공부하다 → 공부해 보다
살다 → 살아 보다	*듣다 → 들어 보다	전화하다 → 전화해 보다

 번지점프를 해 봤어요? Have you ever tried bungee jumping?
한복을 입어 봤어요? Have you tried hanbok?

 Tips

'−아/어 봤어요' is usually indicates an experience in past. It collocates with expressions of frequency, such as once, twice or three times because it expresses an experience.

Vocabulary

한정식 traditional Korean table d'hôte
아직 ~ 아니다 not yet
살다 live
전화하다 make a phone call
번지점프 bungee jumping
한복 hanbok
경복궁 Gyeongbokgung

 **Reviews**

❶ A 투이 씨는 경복궁에 ＿＿＿＿＿＿＿＿? (경복궁에 가다)
Thuy, have you been to Gyeongbokgung?

B 아니요. 시간이 없어서 아직 못 갔어요.
No. I haven't had time to.

 Answers

① 가 봤어요

🎧 MP3 13-05 🎤 MP3 13-06

3

A 그 식당에 꼭 한번 가 보세요.
You have to go to the restaurant.

B 네, 알겠어요. Okay.

★ **verb + −아/어 보다 (2)** (−아/어 보세요)

『Verb + −아/어 보다』is used to make a recommendation. It collocates with expressions of frequency, such as once, twice or three times, because it expresses an experience. 『Verb + −아/어 보다』used to make a suggestion is often combined with '꼭 한번'. This is because 『verb + −아/어 보다』also expresses an attempt.

ex 여기에서는 한정식을 꼭 먹어 보세요.
You have to eat a traditional Korean table d'hôte.

이 옷이 요즘 인기가 참 많아요. 한번 입어 보세요.
This clothes is very popular these days. Try it on.

한강 공원은 참 예뻐요. 한번 가 보세요.
Han River Park is very pretty. You should go there.

Tips

'−아/어 보세요' is used to suggest or recommend that someone try to a certain action.

Vocabulary

식당 restaurant
여기 here
꼭 have to, must
옷 clothes
요즘 these days
인기가 많다 popular
입어 보다 try it on
한강 공원 Han River Park

Reviews

❶ A 제주도는 정말 아름다워요. 꼭 한번 _____.
Jeju Island is very beautiful. You should visit there.

B 네, 저도 가 보고 싶어요. Yes, I want to go, too.

Answers

① 가 보세요

Weekend Activities

소설책을 읽다
read a novel

친구들을 만나다
meet friends

낚시를 가다
go fishing

등산을 하다
go hiking

극장에 가다
go to the theater

맛집에 가다
go to a good restaurant

쇼핑을 가다
go shopping

가구를 만들다
make furniture

그림을 그리다
draw a picture

Dialog

🎧 MP3 13-08 🎤 MP3 13-09

 투이 씨, 이번 주말에 뭐 할 거예요?

 친구하고 같이 인사동에 갈 거예요.

 그래요? 인사동에서 뭐 할 거예요?

 한정식을 먹으러 갈 거예요.

 와, 정말요? 전에도 한정식을 먹어 봤어요?

 아니요, 아직 안 먹어 봤어요.

 그래요? 식당은 예약했어요?

 글쎄요. 아마 친구가 예약했을 거예요.

 그렇군요. 안국역 근처에 한정식 맛집이 있어요.
나중에 거기에서도 꼭 한번 먹어 보세요.

 알겠어요. 고마워요.

이번 this	주말 weekend	인사동 Insadong
한정식 traditional Korean table d'hôte	전에 before	아직 ~ 아니다 not yet
예약하다 make a reservation	아마 maybe, probably	안국역 Anguk Station
근처 near	맛집 a restaurant that is famous for serving delicious food	
나중에 later	꼭 have to, must	

136

Donghyun	Thuy, what are you going to do this weekend?
Thuy	I'm going to Insadong with my friend.
Donghyun	Are you? What are you going to do in Insadong?
Thuy	I'm going to eat traditional Korean table d'hôte.
Donghyun	Wow, really? Have you ever had traditional Korean table d'hôte before?
Thuy	Not yet.
Donghyun	Have you? Did you book a table in a restaurant?
Thuy	I think my friend did.
Donghyun	I see. There is a famous restaurant near Anguk Station. You have to eat there, too.
Thuy	Okay, I'll. Thank you.

1 **Unscramble the given words and read the sentences aloud.**

1 A 어제 뭐 했어요?

   B _____. [카페 / 에 / 갔어요 / 커피 / 를 / 마시러]
     What did you do yesterday? / I went to a café for a coffee.

2 A 주말에 투이 씨를 만날 거예요?

   B 네, _____. [투이 씨 / 하고 / 을 / 밥 / 같이 / 먹을 거예요]
     Are you going to meet Thuy this weekend? / Yes, I'm going to eat out with Thuy.

2 **Fill in the blanks with appropriate words.**

> 번지점프를 하다 / 쇼핑하다 / 친구를 만나다

1 A _____? [–아 / 어 보다]

   B 아니요. 무서워서 아직 안 해 봤어요.
     Have you ever tried bungee jumping? / Not yet. Just thinking of it scares me.

2 A 이번 주말에 뭐 할 거예요?

   B _____. [–(으)ㄹ 거예요]
     What are you going to do this weekend? / I'm going shopping.

3 A 커피숍에 뭐 하러 가요?

   B _____. [–(으)러 가다]
     What are you going to the coffee shop for? / I'm going to meet my friend.

 1 1. 카페에 커피를 마시러 갔어요(커피를 마시러 카페에 갔어요) 2. 투이 씨하고 같이 밥을 먹을 거예요
     2 1. 번지점프를 해 봤어요 2. 쇼핑할 거예요 3. 친구를 만나러 가요

How Korean People Spend Their Leisure Time

Korea is well-known for its top-ranking Internet speed. Though almost every Korean household has two or more computers, Korean people often go to a PC Bang or Internet café, to enjoy a **MMORPG** (Massively Multiplayer Online Role-Playing Game) at a faster speed. They can enjoy games and different

types of food, ranging from snacks to cooked food. Why don't you visit a PC Bang in Korea?

A Korean noraebang (karaoke) is another must-see place. It's easy to find a noraebang in Korea. This is because Korean people love singing. Coin noraebangs, which allow people to sing a song for 500 won, are getting more and more popular these days.

A jjimjilbang (Korean sauna) is a popular place, too. You can experience the ondol, Korea's traditional floor heating system. If you sit or lie on the ondol floor, you may feel too hot at first. However, you'll grow accustomed to the heat and feel comfortable. Once you get used to it, you'll never forget the warmth of the ondol floor. Many jjimjilbangs have a small PC Bang, a cartoon café, a gym, a public bath, a cafeteria, and more.

VR (Virtual Reality) cafés and escape rooms are the latest trends in entertainment. In a VR café, you can get a variety of virtual reality experiences, such as skiing in the mountains, jumping off a high tower, or car racing. In an escape room, you have to escape from the locked room by solving problems given to you within the time limit.

Lesson 14

명동역에 어떻게 가야 돼요?

How can I get to Myeongdong Station?

Key Sentences

1

A 저, 실례합니다. 명동역에 어떻게 가야 돼요?
Excuse me. How can I get to Myeongdong Station?

B 명동역이요? 472번 버스를 타고 가세요.
Myeongdong Station? Take bus number 472.

⭐ 어떻게

'어떻게' (meaning 'how') is used to ask or talk about the way to get somewhere.

ex 학교에 어떻게 와요? How do you get to school?

⭐ verb + ―아/어야 되다(하다)

The pattern 『verb + ―아/어야 되다(하다)』 is used to express an obligation or necessity. When the vowel before '―다' is 'ㅏ' or 'ㅗ', we add '―아야 되다(하다)'. When the vowel before '―다' is not 'ㅏ' or 'ㅗ', we add '―어야 되다(하다)'. When the base form of a verb ends in '하다', we use '해야 되다'. We can also use '―아/어야 하다' instead of '―아/어야 되다'.

동사ㅗ,ㅏ (O) + ―아야 되다	동사ㅗ,ㅏ (X) + ―어야 되다	하다 → 해야 되다
가다 → 가야 되다	마시다 → 마셔야 되다	운동하다 → 운동해야 되다
보다 → 봐야 되다	먹다 → 먹어야 되다	전화하다 → 전화해야 되다

ex 밥을 먹고 30분 후에 약을 먹어야 돼요(해요).
You have to take the medicine 30 minutes after meal.
저는 내일 일을 해야 돼요(해요). I have to work tomorrow.

Reviews

❶ 이건 _____ 마셔요? / 물을 넣고 5분 정도 기다리세요.
How do you drink this? / Pour water and wait about 5 minutes.

❷ 내일 시험이 있어서 _____.
I have an exam tomorrow so I have to study.

Tips

'어떻게 돼요?' is one of the commonly used expressions: '나이가 어떻게 돼요?' (meaning 'how old are you?'), '직업이 어떻게 돼요?' (meaning 'what's your job?'), '형제가 어떻게 돼요?' (meaning 'how many siblings do you have?'), etc.

Vocabulary

실례합니다. Excuse me.
어떻게 how
버스를 타다 take a bus
후에 after
약 medicine
이것 this
넣다 put, pour
정도 about
기다리다 wait
시험 test

Answers

① 어떻게
② 공부해야 돼요(해요)

2

A 여기에서 명동역까지 시간이 얼마나 걸려요?

How long does it take to get to Myeongdong Station from here?

B 버스로 삼십 분쯤 걸려요. It takes about 30 minutes by bus.

★ place + 에서 / place + 까지

『place + 에서』 is used to show the place where someone or something starts, while 『place + 까지』 is used to show the place where someone or something arrives. Therefore, the pattern 『place + 에서 + place + 까지』 corresponds to 'from one place to another' in English.

ex 여기에서 명동까지 택시비가 얼마예요?
How much does it cost to take a taxi from here to Myeongdong?

★ transportation + (으)로

『noun + (으)로』 is used in many different ways depending on what the noun before '(으)로' refers to. If it indicates a place, '(으)로' means 'in the direction of.' If it indicates a vehicle, '(으)로' means by that particular kind of vehicle. When the noun ends in a consonant, we add '으로' but when the noun ends in a vowel or 'ㄹ', we add '로'.

ex 지하철로 한 시간쯤 걸려요. It takes about an hour by subway.
버스는 복잡해요. 택시로 가세요.
The bus is complicated. You'd better take a taxi.

 **Reviews**

❶ 고향에서 한국_____ 시간이 얼마나 걸려요?
How long does it take from your hometown to Korea?

❷ 비행기_____ 5시간쯤 걸려요.
It takes about 5 hours by plane.

 Tips

1. 시간이 얼마나 걸려요? (meaning 'how long does it take ...?') is used to ask about the time spent to travel from one place to another or to finish a job or activity.

2. 『Transportation + (으)로 가다/오다/다니다』 is same as 『transportation + 을/를 타고 가다/오다/다니다』.

ex A 회사에 어떻게 가요?
How do you get to your work?

B 버스를 타고 가요
= 버스로 가요
By bus.

 Vocabulary

여기 here
명동역 Myeongdong
　Station
버스로 by bus
~쯤 about
복잡하다 complicated

Answers

① 까지 ② 로

Lesson 14 명동역에 어떻게 가야 돼요? **143**

🎧 MP3 14-05 🎤 MP3 14-06

3

A 기사님, 여기에서 내리면 돼요?
Excuse me. Can I get off here?

B 명동역에 가지요? 다음에 내리세요.
You're going to Myeongdong Station, right? You get off at the next stop.

⭐ **verb + −(으)면 되다**

'−(으)면 되다' is used to say that if you finish it, you don't have work to do any more. When the verb stem ends in a consonant, '−으면 되다' is added. If the stem ends in a vowel, '−면 되다' is added.

동사 받침 (O) + −으면 되다	동사 ㄹ, 받침 (X) + −면 되다
먹다 → 먹으면 되다	가다 → 가면 되다

ex **A:** 집이 멀어요? Is your house far from here?

B: 아니요. 학교에서 5분 정도만 가면 돼요. No, it is a five-minute walk away.

⭐ **verb/adjective + −지요?**

『verb/adjective + −지요?』 is used to ask for confirmation of the fact that you have known before. Whether the stem ends in a consonant or in a vowel, '지요' is added the stem.

동사/형용사 받침 (O/X) + −지요?	
먹다 → 먹지요?	가다 → 가지요?

ex 오늘 덥지요? Is it hot today?

Reviews

❶ 내일은 회사에 안 _____? / 아니요. 가야 돼요.
You don't go to work tomorrow, do you? / No, I have to go to work.

❷ 문제를 다 풀었지요? / 이것만 _____.
Have you solved all the problems? / This is the only one left.

👜 **Tips**

1. Adjectives can also come before '−(으)면 되다'. It means that's enough if one condition is met. '−(으)면 안 되다' is used to indicate something is forbidden.

ex 화장실에 가고 싶어요. 이쪽으로 가면 돼요? / 아니요. 그쪽으로 가면 안 돼요.
I want to go to the bathroom. Can I go this way? / No, you can't go that way.

2. You can also use the pattern of the 『noun + (이)지요?』. And '−았/었/했지요?' is used for the past tense.

ex 중국 사람이지요?
Are you Chinese?

숙제 다 했지요?
Did you do your homework?

📓 **Vocabulary**

기사 driver
여기 here
내리다 get off
다음 next
문제 problem, question
풀다 solve

Answers

 ① 가지요 ② 풀면 돼요

144

Transportation

버스
bus

지하철
subway

기차
train

택시
taxi

오토바이
motorcycle

자전거
bicycle

자동차
car

비행기
plane

배
ship

트럭
truck

구급차
ambulance

헬리콥터
helicopter

Dialog

🎧 MP3 14-08 🎤 MP3 14-09

 저, 실례합니다. 강남역에 어떻게 가야 돼요?

 145번 버스를 타고 가세요.

 감사합니다.

...

 기사님, 이 버스 강남역에 가요?

 네, 가요.

 시간이 얼마나 걸려요?

 20분쯤 걸려요.

...

 여기에서 내리면 돼요?

 아니요. 다음에 내리세요.

실례합니다. Excuse me.	강남역 Gangnam Station	어떻게 how
버스를 타다 take a bus	기사 driver	시간 time
얼마나 how	걸리다 take	~쯤 about
여기 here	내리다 get off	다음 next

146

Thuy	Excuse me. How can I get to Gangnam Station?
Passenger	Take bus number 145.
Thuy	Thank you.

· · ·

Thuy	Excuse me. Is this bus going to Gangnam Station?
Driver	Yes, it is.
Thuy	How long does it take to get there?
Driver	It takes about 20 minutes.

· · ·

| Thuy | Can I get off here? |
| Driver | No. You get off at the next stop. |

1 Fill in the blanks and say the sentences aloud.

1 A 동현 씨는 학교에 어떻게 와요?
      How do you come to school, Donghyun?

   B _____ . [버스]
      I come here by bus.

2 A 강남역에 가고 싶어요. 버스를 _____?
      I want to go to Gangnam Station. Can I go there by bus?

   B 버스는 안 가요. 지하철을 타세요.
      No, there is no bus going there near here. Take the subway.

2 Fill in the blanks in the dialog with appropriate words.

> 강남역 / 가다 / 버스 / 타다

1 A 저기요. 273번 버스가 _____ 에 가지요?
      Excuse me. Is bus number 273 going to Gangnam Station, right?

   B 네, 그런데 조금 멀어요. 지하철을 타세요.
      Yes, but it'll take longer. You'd better take the subway.

2 A 이 버스 인사동에 _____?
      Is this bus going to Insadong?

   B 네.
      Yes, it is.

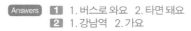 **1** 1. 버스로 와요 2. 타면 돼요
          2 1. 강남역 2. 가요

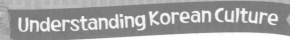

Korea's Subway System and Transfer Transportation Services

Korea's public transportation fares are relatively low. In addition, the transfer transportation services are well-organized; you can transfer from local bus to subway, subway to local bus, or bus to bus at little or no extra cost.

The T-money card is the most commonly used transit card and can be recharged in subway stations or convenience stores. Furthermore, you can enjoy a selection of several uniquely designed cards.

The subway system around Seoul is so complicated and confusing that you should be careful which line you take. Never forget to scan your card when you get on or off; otherwise, you will pay more.

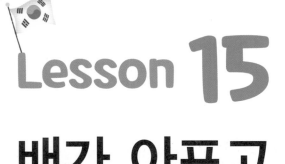

Lesson 15

배가 아프고 소화가 안 돼요.

I have indigestion and stomach pain.

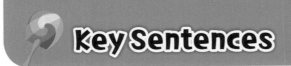

Key Sentences

1

A 어떻게 오셨어요? What brings you here today?

B 배가 아프고 소화가 안 돼요.
I have indigestion and stomach pain.

★ Body and symptoms

얼굴	얼굴, 머리, 눈, 코, 입, 귀			
몸	목, 어깨, 팔, 손, 가슴, 배, 허리, 엉덩이, 다리, 무릎, 발			
아프다	열이 나다	감기에 걸리다	기침이 나다	배가 아프다
배탈이 나다	소화가 안 되다	토하다	설사를 하다	다치다
피가 나다	연고를 바르다	약을 먹다	소독하다	밴드를 붙이다

★ What brings you here?

The expression '어떻게 오셨어요?' has two different meanings. First, it can mean 'How did you get here?', which is a question about the listener's means of transportation. Second, it can mean 'What brings you here?', which is a question about the purpose of the listener's visit.

ex (병원) 어떻게 오셨어요? / 배가 아파서 왔어요.
What brings you here? / I have a stomachache.

 Tips

1. Use '어디' when you need to ask what parts of body — such as the head, eyes, nose, mouth, and ears — ache.

   ex 어디가 아프세요?
   Where does it hurt?

2. When someone asks about the purpose of your visit, Korean people doesn't say '뭐 하러 오셨어요?' (meaning 'what did you come here for?'). Instead, they usually say, '어떻게 오셨어요' (meaning 'what brings you here?').

 Vocabulary

어떻게 how
배가 아프다 have a stomachache
소화가 안 되다 indigestion
병원 hospital
머리가 아프다 have a headache
기침하다 cough

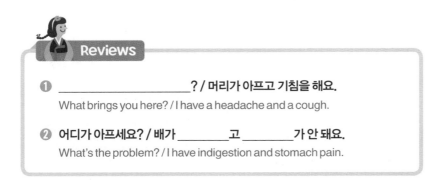

Reviews

❶ _____? / 머리가 아프고 기침을 해요.
What brings you here? / I have a headache and a cough.

❷ 어디가 아프세요? / 배가 _____고 _____가 안 돼요.
What's the problem? / I have indigestion and stomach pain.

 Answers

① 어떻게 오셨어요
② 아프/소화

2

A 이 약을 하루에 세 번, 식사 후에 드세요.
Take this medicine three times a day after each meal.

B 밥을 먹어도 돼요? Can I have a meal?

★ verb + −아/어도 되다

The pattern of 『verb + −아/어도 되다』 is used to ask for permission. When the vowel before '−다' is 'ㅏ' or 'ㅗ', we add '−아도 되다'. When the vowel before '−다' is not 'ㅏ' or 'ㅗ', we add '−어도 되다'. When the base form of a verb ends in '하다', we use '해도 되다'.

동사 ㅗ, ㅏ (O) + −아도 되다	동사 ㅗ, ㅏ (X) + −어도 되다	하다 → 해도 되다
가다 → 가도 되다	마시다 → 마셔도 되다	운동하다 → 운동해도 되다
보다 → 봐도 되다	먹다 → 먹어도 되다	전화하다 → 전화해도 되다
만나다 → 만나도 되다	읽다 → 읽어도 되다	청소하다 → 청소해도 되다
놀다 → 놀아도 되다	*듣다 → 들어도 되다	빨래하다 → 빨래해도 되다

ex 여기에 들어가도 돼요? / 아니요, 들어가면 안 돼요.
Can I enter here? / No. You can't go inside.

여기에서 사진을 찍어도 돼요? / 네, 찍어도 돼요.
Can I take a picture here? / Yes, you can take a picture.

 Tips

In case of a noun, '후에' or '전에' is comes right after the noun.

ex 매일 10시 전에 자요.
I go to bed before 10 o'clock every day.

Vocabulary

약 medicine
하루 day
식사 meal
후에 after
들어가다 enter
사진을 찍다 take a picture

 **Reviews**

❶ **A** 여기에서 사진을 _____?
Can I take photos here?

B 여기에서 사진을 찍으면 안 돼요.
You cannot take photos here.

 Answers

① 찍어도 돼요

Key Sentences

 MP3 15-05   MP3 15-06

3

A 소화가 안 되니까 죽을 드세요.

Have soup because you have indigestion.

B 네, 알겠습니다. Okay.

★ verb/adjective + –(으)니까

'–(으)니까' is used to connect clauses of cause and result. The reason the pharmacist says 'Have soup' is that someone has indigestion. Since it expresses a subjective reason, '–(으)니까' is rarely used in writing. When the verb or adjective stem ends in a consonant, '–으니까' is added. When the stem ends in a vowel and '–ㄹ', '–니까' is added. If it is added to a noun, the form 『noun + (이)니까』 is used.

동사/형용사 받침 (O) + –으니까	동사/형용사 ㄹ, 받침 (X) + –니까
먹다 → 먹으니까	가다 → 가니까
읽다 → 읽으니까	하다 → 하니까
*듣다 → 들으니까	크다 → 크니까
*어렵다 → 어려우니까	*놀다 → 노니까

ex 우리 날씨가 좋으니까 같이 놀러 가요. (O) 우리 날씨가 좋아서 같이 놀러 가요. (X)
The weather is nice, so let's go outside.

길이 막히니까 지하철을 타세요. (O) 길이 막혀서 지하철을 타세요. (X)
Take the subway because the road is blocked.

Reviews

❶ 같이 쇼핑할까요? / 내일은 시험이 _____ 다음에 같이 가요.

Do you want to go shopping together? / I have a test tomorrow so let's go together next time.

❷ 오늘 날씨가 _____ 점퍼를 입으세요.

It's cold today, wear a jumper.

 Tips

Unlike '–아/어서', '–(으)니까' has a past tense form: when the vowel before '–다' is 'ㅏ' or 'ㅗ', we add '–았으니까' but when the vowel before '–다' is not 'ㅏ' or 'ㅗ', we add '–었으니까'. When the stem ends in '–하다', we use '–했으니까'.

Vocabulary

소화가 안 되다 indigestion
죽 soup, porridge
날씨 weather
길이 막히다 a road is blocked
점퍼 jumper, jacket

 Answers

① 있으니까 ② 추우니까

154

'己'Drop

🎧 MP3 15-07

When the verb of adjective stem, which ends in the consonant '己' combined to the verb endings that starts with 'ㄴ, ㅂ, ㅅ' or '己', the final consonant '己' of the stem is dropped.

기본형(사전형)	–아/어요	–았/었어요	–(으)ㄹ 거예요	–고
만들다	만들어요	만들었어요	만들 거예요	만들고
놀다	놀아요	놀았어요	놀 거예요	놀고
불다	불어요	불었어요	불 거예요	불고
살다	살아요	살았어요	살 거예요	살고
길다	길어요	길었어요	길 거예요	길고
멀다	멀어요	멀었어요	멀 거예요	멀고
달다	달아요	달았어요	달 거예요	달고
힘들다	힘들어요	힘들었어요	힘들 거예요	힘들고

기본형(사전형)	–지만	–(으)세요	–(으)러 가다	–(으)니까
만들다	만들지만	만드세요	만들러 가다	만드니까
놀다	놀지만	노세요	놀러 가다	노니까
불다	불지만	부세요		부니까
살다	살지만	사세요	살러 가다	사니까
길다	길지만			기니까
멀다	멀지만			머니까
달다	달지만			다니까
힘들다	힘들지만			힘드니까

Dialog

🎧 MP3 15-08　🎤 MP3 15-09

 어떻게 오셨어요?

 머리가 아프고 열이 나요.

 언제부터 열이 났어요?

 어제 저녁부터 났어요.

 콧물도 나고 기침도 해요?

 콧물은 안 나지만 목이 아프고 기침도 해요.

 아마 감기일 거예요.
이 약을 하루에 세 번, 식사 후에 드세요.

 그런데 병원에 안 가도 돼요?

 심하지 않으니까 괜찮을 거예요.
우선 무리하지 말고 푹 쉬세요.

 네, 알겠습니다. 감사합니다.

어떻게 오셨어요? What brings you here?	머리가 아프다 have a headache	열이 나다 have a fever
언제 when	콧물이 나다 have a runny nose	기침하다 cough
목이 아프다 have a sore throat	아마 maybe, probably	감기 cold
약 medicine	식사 meal	후에 after
그런데 by the way	심하다 bad, heavy, severe	무리하다 work too hard
푹 쉬다 have a good rest		

Pharmacist	What brings you here?
Thuy	I have a headache and a fever.
Pharmacist	How long have you had a fever?
Thuy	Since last night.
Pharmacist	Do you have a runny nose and a cough?
Thuy	I don't have a runny nose, but I do have a sore throat and a cough.
Pharmacist	You seem to have a cold.
	Take this medicine three times a day after each meal.
Thuy	By the way, do I have to go to the hospital?
Pharmacist	Since your symptoms are not so bad, you'll be okay.
	Don't work too hard and have a good rest.
Thuy	Okay. Thank you.

Exercises

1 Fill in the blanks and say the sentences aloud.

어제 길에서 넘어졌어요. 그래서 다리를 _____ .

피가 나서 약국에 갔어요. 약사가 _____를 줬어요.

그래서 연고를 _____ . 그리고 밴드를 _____ .

Yesterday, I fell on the street and hurt my leg. My leg was bleeding. I went to the drugstore. The pharmacist told me to apply ointment on the wound. So I applied some ointment and put a bandage on it.

2 Fill in the blanks.

1   A   어떻게 오셨어요?

    B   머리가 아프고 _____이 나요.
       What brings you here? / I have a headache and a fever.

2   A   여기에 들어가도 돼요?

    B   출입금지니까 _____.
       Can I go in there? / You shouldn't go in there because the area is off limits.

3   A   약을 먹어야 돼요?

    B   네, 이 약을 식사 ___에 드세요.
       Should I take this medicine? / Yes, take this medicine after meal.

 Answers   **1** 다쳤어요/연고/발랐어요/붙였어요
             2 1. 열 2. 들어가지 마세요 3. 후

Signs

출입 금지
들어가지 마세요.
들어가면 안 돼요.

DO NOT ENTER

사진 촬영 금지
사진을 찍지 마세요.
사진을 찍으면 안 돼요.

No Photography

휴대폰 사용 금지
휴대폰을 사용하지 마세요.
휴대폰을 사용하면 안 돼요.

No Cell Phone Use

낙서 금지
낙서하지 마세요.
낙서하면 안 돼요.

No Scribbling

음식물 반입 금지
음식물을 가지고 들어오지 마세요.
음식을 가지고 들어오면 안 돼요.

No Food or Drink Allowed

금연
담배를 피우지 마세요.
담배를 피우면 안 돼요.

No Smoking

주차 금지
주차를 하지 마세요.
주차를 하면 안 돼요.

No Parking

손대지 마세요
손을 대지 마세요.
손을 대면 안 돼요.

Do Not Touch

애완동물 출입 금지
애완동물을 데리고 들어오지 마세요.
애완동물을 데리고 들어오면 안 돼요.

No Pets Allowed

Lesson 16

너는 시간 있을 때 보통 뭐 해?

What do you usually do when you're free?

Key Sentences

1

A 마이클, 너는 시간 있을 때 보통 뭐 해?

Michael, what do you do in your free time?

B 내 취미는 수영이야. 그래서 보통 수영장에 가.

My hobby is swimming. So I usually go to the pool when I'm free.

⭐ Casual Speech (1)

In the Korean language, there are two ways of speaking: honorific and humble forms which is called '존댓말', and informal or casual form, which is called '반말'. Whether to use '존댓말' or '반말' depends on the age gap or intimacy between the speaker and the listener. When we converse with close friends, we use '반말', in which the verb or adjective ending doesn't end in '–요'.

동사			형용사		
기본형	반말(현재)	반말(과거)	기본형	반말(현재)	반말(과거)
가다	가	갔어	예쁘다	예뻐	예뻤어
읽다	읽어	읽었어	좋다	좋아	좋았어

⭐ Casual Speech (2) → noun + (이)야

In Lesson 4, we studied the pattern of 『noun + 이에요/예요』. In casual speech, we say 『noun + (이)야』.

ex 너는 취미가 뭐야? / 내 취미는 운동이야.
What is your hobby? / My hobby is exercise.

Reviews

❶ 아빠, 이 친구가 마이클이에요. / 안녕? 만나서 _____.
Dad, this is Michael. / Hello. Nice to meet you.

❷ 안녕? 내 이름은 투이_____. / 내 이름은 양양이야.
Hello? My name is Thuy. / My name is Yangyang.

Tips

1. When you talk using '반말', you should say '나' if you refer to yourself (the speaker) instead of '저'. Use '너' when you address someone you're talking to.

2. 『Verb/Adjective + –(으)ㄹ 거야』 is used for expectations or speculations about a future event or state. In addition, we can use 『verb + –(으)ㄹ 거야』 as a future form of the verb.

Vocabulary

보통 usually
취미 hobby
수영 swimming
수영장 pool
아빠 dad

Answers

① 반가워 ② 야

162

2

A 마이클, 내일 수영장에 갈 거야?
Michael, are you going to the pool tomorrow?

B 응, (우리) 같이 갈까?   Sure. Would you like to join me?

★ Casual Speech (3)

→ verb/adjective + −(으)ㄹ래, −(으)ㄹ까?, −지?, −고 싶어

In the previous lessons, we studied '−(으)ㄹ래요', '−(으)ㄹ까요?', '−지요?' and '−고 싶어요' attached to the verb or adjective stem. If you drop '요', you can use these verb endings in casual speech.

ex 뭐 먹을래? / 나는 김밥하고 떡볶이를 먹을래.
What do you want to eat? / I want to eat gimbap and tteokbokki.

뭐 하고 싶어? / 나는 영화를 보고 싶어.
What do you want to do? / I want to see a movie.

★ Casual Speech (4) → verb + −자

『Verb + −자』 is used to make a suggestion. 『(우리) (같이) verb + −아/어』 is another expression of suggestion, which is used as the 『(우리) (같이) verb + −아/어요』 pattern in informal polite speech.

ex 우리 학교에 가자. Let's go to school.

이거 같이 먹자. Let's eat this together.

Reviews

❶ 이번 주말에 뭐 _____? (하다) / 집에서 _____. (쉬다)
What are you going to do this weekend? / I'll have a rest at home.

❷ 내일 몇 시에 _____? (만나다) / 오후 다섯 시가 어때?
What time shall we meet tomorrow? / How about five o'clock?

 Tips

1. In casual speech, 'yes' corresponds to '응' and 'no' corresponds to '아니'. In formal speech, we say '네' or '아니요'.

2. 『Verb + −(으)세요』 in informal −polite speech is changed to 『Verb + −아/어』 in casual speech. Be careful not to say 『Verb + −(으)세』.

3. Since the pattern of 『Verb + 아/어』 is used for different purposes −command, suggestion, and declaration−, be careful with its intonation when you say the pattern of 『verb+아/어』.

 Vocabulary

내일 tomorrow
수영장 pool
이것 this
주말 weekend
쉬다 take a rest
오후 afternoon

Answers

① 할 거야/쉴 거야   ② 만날까?

Key Sentences

3

A 투이, 너도 수영할 수 있지? 같이 가자.

Thuy, can you swim, too? Let's go together.

B 미안. 나는 못 가. 어제 고향에서 친구가 왔어.

Sorry. I can't. One of my friends came from hometown to see me.

★ verb + −(으)ㄹ 수 있다/없다

『Verb + −(으)ㄹ 수 있다/없다』 has two different meanings: one is expressing ability and the other is expressing possibility. When the verb stem ends in any consonant excluding 'ㄹ', '−을 수 있다' or '−을 수 없다' is added. When the verb stem ends in the consonant 'ㄹ' or a vowel, '−ㄹ 수 있다' or '−ㄹ 수 없다' is added. If 『verb + −(으)ㄹ 수 있다/없다』 expresses possibility, it indicates that something is possible or impossible.

동사 받침 (O) + −을 수 있다/없다		동사 받침 (X), ㄹ + ㄹ 수 있다/없다	
먹다	먹을 수 있다/없다	가다	갈 수 있다/없다

ex 수영 할 수 있어요? / 네, 할 수 있어요. Can you swim? / Yes, I can.

★ 못 + verb

In the pattern of 『못 + verb』, '못' means the speaker cannot do something because the circumstances do not allow it.

ex 김치를 좋아해요? / 아니요. 너무 매워서 못 먹어요. (*못 좋아해요(X))
Do you like kimchi? / No. It's so spicy that I can't eat it.

Reviews

❶ 어제 옷 많이 샀어? / 아니. 옷이 안 예뻐서 그냥 _____.

Did you buy lots of clothes? / No, I didn't. I didn't like any of them.

❷ 너는 피아노를 _____? / 아니, _____.

Can you play the piano? / No, I can't play the piano.

Vocabulary

못 can't
고향 hometown
김치 kimchi
너무 so, too
맵다 spicy
옷 clothes
피아노를 치다 play the piano

Answers

① 안 샀어
② 칠 수 있어/칠 수 없어 (못 쳐)

Hobby

🎧 MP3 16-07

운동을 하다
exercise, work out

수영을 하다
swim

태권도를 하다
do taekwondo

농구를 하다
play basketball

축구를 하다
play soccer

요가를 하다
do yoga

스키를 타다
ski

스케이트를 타다
skate

보드를 타다
ride a skateboard

당구를 치다
play billiards

테니스를 치다
play tennis

배드민턴을 치다
play badminton

악기를 연주하다
play a musical instrument

드럼을 치다
play the drums

기타를 치다
play the guitar

피아노를 치다
play the piano

바이올린을 켜다
play the violin

첼로를 켜다
play cello

그림을 그리다
paint/draw (a picture)

노래를 부르다
sing a song

영화를 보다
watch a movie

책을 읽다
read a book

음악을 듣다
listen to music

사진을 찍다
take a picture

🎧 MP3 16-08 🎤 MP3 16-09

 투이, 너는 시간이 있을 때 보통 뭐 해?

 나는 보통 영화를 봐. 너는?

 나는 운동을 해. 운동이 내 취미야.

 마이클, 너도 운동을 좋아하지?

 응, 나는 시간이 있을 때 보통 수영장에 가.
고향에서는 매일 수영을 했어.

 그럼 내일 수영하러 갈까?

 그래, 같이 가자. 투이, 너도 갈래?

 나도 같이 가고 싶지만 수영을 못 해.

 괜찮아. 금방 배울 수 있을 거야.

보통 usually	영화를 보다 watch movies	운동을 하다 play sports
취미 hobby	수영장 pool	고향 hometown
매일 every day	금방 soon, shortly	배우다 learn

Donghyun	Thuy, what do you do in your free time?
Thuy	I usually watch movies. How about you?
Donghyun	I play sports. Playing sports is my hobby.
Thuy	Michael, do you like playing sports, too?
Michael	Yes, I usually go swimming when I have free time. I used to go swimming every day in my hometown.
Donghyun	Then should we go swimming tomorrow?
Michael	Sure. Thuy, you'll join us, won't you?
Thuy	I'd like to, but I don't know how to swim.
Michael	Don't worry. You'll learn fast.

1 Fill in the blanks and say the sentences aloud.

1

A 네 취미는 뭐야?

B 내 _____은/는 _____(이)야.
What is your hobby? / My hobby is swimming.

2

A _____이/가 있을 때 보통 뭐 해?

B 나는 보통 _____을/를 들어.
What do you do in your free time? / I usually listen to music.

2 Fill in the blanks.

1 A 김치찌개 먹을까?

B 아니, 난 김치찌개는 너무 매워서 _____. [먹다]
Why don't we have kimchi jjiggae? / I'm sorry. I can't eat kimchi jjiggae because it's so spicy.

2 A 시간이 _____ 보통 뭐 해? [있다]

B 나는 보통 _____. [요리를 하다]
What do you do in your free time? / I usually cook.

3 A 와인 한 잔 마실래요?

B 아니요. 저는 알레르기가 있어서 술을 _____ 마셔요.
Would you like a glass of wine? / No. I can't drink because I'm allergic to alcohol.

Answers **1** 1. 취미/수영 2. 시간/음악
2 1. 못 먹어(= 먹을 수 없어) 2. 있을 때/요리를 해 3. 못

Formal Speech and Informal Speech

In this lesson we've studied the two ways of speaking in Korean: '존댓말' and '반말'. Korean people use '존댓말' or '반말' depending on the age gap or relationship between the speaker and the listener. You can speak in '반말' to someone who is a lot younger than you — especially to children —, to someone of the same age as you, or to someone who has an intimate relationship with you. However, it's not desirable to speak in '반말' before you have a close friendship with someone, even if the person you're talking to is younger than you or the same age of you. Also, lots of children speak in '반말' to their parents, but talking like this in public sounds rude.

Remember that you should speak in '존댓말' to elder people. Korean people use '존댓말' to show respect for elder people, such as your grandparents, parents, boss or customer. As you know, '저' is a personal pronoun used in formal speech while '나' is used in informal speech.

Lesson 17

복습 문제

Review

1 **Choose the dialog that sounds natural.**

① A: 주말에 시간이 있어요?   B: 미안해요. 금요일은 바빠요.

② A: 언제 만날까요?   B: 명동역이 어때요?

③ A: 토요일에 만나요.   B: 네, 그럼 여섯 시에 명동역에서 만나요.

④ A: 어디에서 만날까요?   B: 오후에 만나요.

2 **Choose the appropriate word for the blank.**

A _____ 뭐 했어요?

B 친구하고 같이 영화를 봤어요.

① 어제   ② 내일

③ 모레   ④ 주말

3 **Choose the correct answer to the given question.**

A 몇 월 며칠이에요?

B _____ 이에요.

A 무슨 요일이에요?

B _____ 이에요.

① 십 월 십육 일 / 월요일

② 시 월 십육 일 / 화요일

③ 십 월 십육 일 / 수요일

④ 시 월 십육 일 / 금요일

4 **Choose the appropriate word for the blank.**

A _____ 한국에 왔어요?

B 한국어를 공부하러 왔어요.

① 왜   ② 언제

③ 어디   ④ 어떻게

5 **Choose one word that is appropriate for both blanks.**

A _____ 오셨어요?

B 배가 아프고 소화가 안 돼요.

A 명동에 _____ 가요?

B 101번 버스를 타고 가요.

① 왜   ② 언제

③ 어디   ④ 어떻게

6 Look at the picture and choose the appropriate word for the blank.

A 친구를 _____ 뭐 했어요?	① 봐서 ② 가서
B 같이 영화를 봤어요.	③ 만나서 ④ 일어나서

7 Choose which one is grammatically incorrect.

① 먹다 → 먹을 거예요   ② 쓰다 → 쓸 거예요   ③ 덥다 → 더울 거예요   ④ 놀다 → 놀을 거예요

8 Choose which one is grammatically incorrect.

① 어렵다 → 어려웠어요   ② 귀엽다 → 귀여웠어요   ③ 입다 → 입었어요   ④ 눕다 → 눕었어요

9 Choose the appropriate word for the blank.

A 어디에 갈 거예요?	① 읽어요 ② 읽었어요
B 도서관에 가서 책을 _____.	③ 읽을까요 ④ 읽을 거예요

10 Choose the appropriate response to the given question.

A 영화가 어땠어요?	① 재미있었어요 ② 더웠어요
B _____.	③ 귀여웠어요 ④ 예뻤어요

11 Choose where this conversation would most likely to take place.

A 어떻게 오셨어요?	① 우체국 ② 약국
B 열이 나고 기침을 해요.	③ 도서관 ④ 마트

12 Choose the appropriate word for the blank.

A 마이클, 시간이 있을 때 보통 뭐 해?
B 나는 보통 _____.

① 사진을 찍을 거야
② 사진을 찍었어
③ 사진을 찍을래
④ 사진을 찍으러 가

13 Choose the appropriate word for the blank.

A 한국 책을 _____?
B 네, _____.

① 읽어 봤어요 　② 읽어 보세요
③ 읽어 볼까요 　④ 읽지 마세요

14 Choose one grammatically correct sentence.

① 다음 주에 공부했어요. 　② 어제 고향에 갈 거예요.
③ 아침부터 저녁까지 공부했어요. 　④ 고향에서 한국까지 시간이 한 시간 많아요.

15 Choose the appropriate word for the blank.

A 투이, 오늘 양양을 만나?
B 아니. 일이 바빠서 _____ 만나.

① 자주 　② 가끔
③ 못 　④ 전혀

16 Choose the appropriate word for the blank.

A 밥을 먹어도 돼요?
B 네, _____.

① 먹었어요 　② 먹어도 돼요
③ 먹으면 안 돼요 　④ 먹지 마세요

17 Choose one grammatically <u>incorrect</u> sentence.

① 린다 씨는 예쁘고 귀여워요.

② 동현 씨는 매일 공부하지만 공부를 못 해요.

③ 백화점은 비싸니까 저는 백화점에서 옷을 안 사요.

④ 저는 아침에 바빠서 아침을 먹지 말고 점심을 드세요.

18 Choose the appropriate word for the blank.

A 몇 번 버스를 _____?
B 160번 버스를 타세요.

① 탔어요　② 탈 거예요

③ 타도 돼요　④ 타야 돼요

19 Choose the appropriate word for the blank.

A 내일 같이 영화 _____?
B 응, 좋아.

① 보지 않아　② 볼 수 없지

③ 보러 갈까　④ 보고 싶어 해

20 Put the sentences in order in order to make a natural dialog.

① 동현 씨, 주말에 시간이 있어요?

② 일요일은 바쁘지만 토요일은 괜찮아요.

③ 오후 여섯 시가 어때요?

④ 그럼 토요일에 같이 영화를 봐요.

⑤ 좋아요. 몇 시에 만날까요?

⑥ 네, 그럼 오후 여섯 시에 영화관 앞에서 만나요.

⑦ 네, 좋아요. 그럼 토요일에 만나요.

① ➡ _____ ➡ _____ ➡ ⑤ ➡ _____ ➡ _____ ➡ ⑦

Answers　1. ③　2. ①　3. ④　4. ①　5. ④　6. ③　7. ④　8. ④　9. ④　10. ①
11. ②　12. ④　13. ①　14. ③　15. ③　16. ②　17. ④　18. ④　19. ③　20. ②④③⑥

나 혼자 끝내는 독학 한국어 첫걸음

Super Easy Korean for Beginners:
A Self-Study Book

Word Lists + Picture Words

넥서스

Word
Lists

저는 I'm

제 이름 my name

학생 student

기자 reporter

의사 doctor

경찰 policeman

어느 which

나라 country

베트남 Vietnam

학교 school

우리 our

교실 classroom

유학생
international student

아니요 no

네 yes

미국 사람 American

베트남 사람 Vietnamese

일본 사람 Japanese

안녕하세요. Hello.

책 book

가방 bag

펜 pen

지우개 eraser

직업 job

선생님 teacher

핸드폰 cellular phone

시계 watch

집 house

친구 friend

공책 notebook

반 친구 classmate

학교 school

미국 America

이거(이것) this

그거(그것) it

한국어 책 Korean book

누구의 whose

그럼 then

저거(저것) that

3

학생 식당
students' cafeteria

회사 work

집 home

학교 school

방 room

건물 building

근처 near

공원 park

앞 in front of

책상 desk

위 on

가방 bag

지갑 wallet

여기 here

저기 there

친구 friend

책 book

커피숍 coffee shop

식당 restaurant

어디 where

옆 next to

도서관 library

4

지금 now	슈퍼마켓 supermarket
책 book	물 water
읽다 read	사다 buy
살다 live	빵 bread
가다 go	재미있다 fun
먹다 eat, have	어렵다 difficult
마시다 drink	많다 many, much
공부하다 study	싸다 cheap
운동하다 work out	적다 few, little
보다 see	따뜻하다 warm
만나다 meet	시원하다 cool
편지 letter	매일 every day
쓰다 write	맛있다 delicious
어디 where	비싸다 expensive
도서관 library	학교 school
자다 sleep	친구 friend

5

그리고 and

영화관 theater

그렇지만 but

강남역 Gangnam station

근처 near

음식 food	라면 ramen
먹다 eat, have	주문 order
듣다 listen	그릇 bowl
읽다 read	공책 notebook
가다 go	지우개 eraser
쓰다 write	친구 friend
쉬다 take a rest	비빔밥 bibimbap
오늘 today	잠시만 for a moment
PC방 Internet café	기다리다 wait
떡볶이 tteokbokki	맛 taste
김밥 gimbap	맵다 spicy
만들다 make	그렇지만 but
마시다 drink	맛있다 delicious
우유 milk	
콜라 coke	
맥주 beer	

Lesson 09

방 room

청소하다 clean

쉬다 take a rest

많다 a lot

만나다 meet

맛있다 delicious

마시다 drink

피곤하다 tired

운동하다 work out

작다 small

예쁘다 pretty

쉽다 easy

재미있다 fun

세수하다 wash one's face

바로 immediately

씻다 wash

공부 study

많이 a lot

시험 성적 grade

열심히 hard

숙제를 하다
do one's homework

야근을 하다 work overtime

어제 yesterday

일어나다 get up

공부하다 study

혼자 alone

친구 friend

늦게 late

Lesson 10

크리스마스 Christmas

들어오다 enter, come in

들어가다 enter, come in

나오다 come out

나가다 get out

올라오다 come up

올라가다 go up

내려오다 come down

내려가다 go down

층 floor

지금 now

시 hour

분 minute

30분 half - hour

가족 family

전화번호 phone number

사무실 office

생일 파티 birthday party

참 Oh

초대하다 invite

잠깐만요. Wait a minute.

아직 yet

Lesson 11

주말 weekend

바쁘다 busy

그렇지만 but

키가 크다 tall

키가 작다 short

자전거 bike

옷 clothes

비싸다 expensive

오후 afternoon

머리가 아프다
have a headache

병원 hospital

기분이 좋다 feel good

명동역
Myeongdong Station

만나다 meet

쉬다 have a rest

듣다 listen

비빔밥 bibimbap

시간이 있다 have time

다음 주 next week

오전 morning

괜찮다 okay, fine

명동역
Myeongdong Station

출구 exit

10

Lesson 12

요즘 these days

덥다 hot

비가 오다/내리다 rain

날씨 weather

따뜻하다 warm

시원하다 cool

바람이 불다 windy

춥다 cold

눈이 오다/내리다 snow

김치찌개 kimchi stew

여름 summer

내일 tomorrow

여자 친구 girlfriend

맑다 sunny, clear

음식 food

맛있다 delicious

공부하다 study

계절 season

봄 spring

따뜻하다 warm

꽃 flower

피다 bloom

덥다 hot

장마철 the rainy season

필요하다 need

우산 umbrella

챙기다 take

11

주말 weekend	경복궁 Gyeongbokgung
한정식 traditional Korean table d'hôte	식당 restaurant
인사동 Insadong	여기 here
다음 주 next week	꼭 have to, must
편지 letter	옷 clothes
보내다 send	요즘 these days
우체국 post office	인기가 많다 popular
도서관 library	입어 보다 try it on
공부하다 study	한강 공원 Han River Park
아직 ~ 아니다 not yet	이번 this
살다 live	전에 before
전화하다 make a phone call	예약하다 make a reservation
번지점프 bungee jumping	아마 maybe, probably
한복 hanbok	안국역 Anguk Station
	근처 near

맛집
a restaurant that is
famous for serving
delicious food

나중에 later

Lesson 14

실례합니다. Excuse me.	**기사** driver
어떻게 how	**내리다** get off
버스를 타다 take a bus	**다음** next
후에 after	**문제** problem, question
약 medicine	**풀다** solve
이것 this	**강남역** Gangnam Station
넣다 put, pour	**시간** time
정도 about	**얼마나** how
기다리다 wait	**걸리다** take
시험 test	
여기 here	
명동역 Myeongdong Station	
버스로 by bus	
~쯤 about	
복잡하다 complicated	

Lesson 15

어떻게 how

배가 아프다
have a stomachache

소화가 안 되다 indigestion

병원 hospital

머리가 아프다
have a headache

기침하다 cough

약 medicine

하루 day

식사 meal

후에 after

들어가다 enter

사진을 찍다 take a picture

죽 soup, porridge

날씨 weather

길이 막히다
a road is blocked

점퍼 jumper, jacket

어떻게 오셨어요?
What brings you here?

열이 나다 have a fever

언제 when

콧물이 나다
have a runny nose

목이 아프다
have a sore throat

아마 maybe, probably

감기 cold

그런데 by the way

심하다 bad, heavy, severe

무리하다 work too hard

푹 쉬다 have a good rest

보통 usually

취미 hobby

수영 swimming

수영장 pool

아빠 dad

내일 tomorrow

이것 this

주말 weekend

쉬다 take a rest

오후 afternoon

못 can't

고향 hometown

김치 kimchi

너무 so, too

맵다 spicy

옷 clothes

피아노를 치다
play the piano

영화를 보다 watch movies

운동을 하다 play sports

매일 every day

금방 soon, shortly

배우다 learn

16

Picture
Words

01 Family

 할아버지
grandfather

 할머니
grandmother

 아버지
father

 어머니
mother

 고모(이모)
aunt

 (외)삼촌
uncle

 형(오빠), 남동생
brother

 누나(언니), 여동생
sister

19

🎧 MP3 W2-02

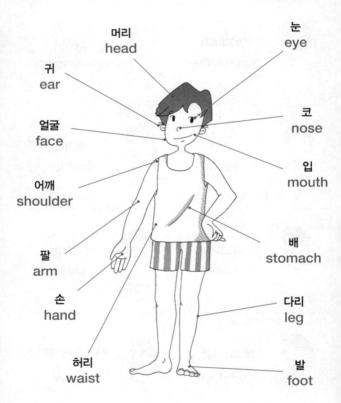

머리
head

눈
eye

귀
ear

코
nose

얼굴
face

입
mouth

어깨
shoulder

팔
arm

배
stomach

손
hand

다리
leg

허리
waist

발
foot

한국
Korea

일본
Japan

중국
China

독일
Germany

미국
U.S.
(the United States)

프랑스
France

영국
U.K.
(the United Kingdom)

캐나다
Canada

이탈리아
Italy

스위스
Switzerland

스웨터
sweater

 티셔츠
T-shirt

 바지
pants

 청바지
jeans

 스커트, 치마
skirt

 원피스, 드레스
dress

 캡, 모자
cap

 양말
socks

 장갑
gloves

텔레비전
television

다리미
iron

냉장고
refrigerator

선풍기
fan

디지털카메라
digital camera

헤어드라이어
hairdryer

진공청소기
vacuum
cleaner

밥솥
rice cooker

세탁기
washing machine

나이프
knife

스푼, 숟가락
spoon

포크
fork

젓가락
chopsticks

접시
plate

컵
cup

주전자
kettle

MP3 W2-07

가방
bag

책상
desk

의자
chair

칠판
blackboard

교과서
textbook

노트
notebook

연필
pencil

지우개
eraser

펜
pen

콜라
Coke

차
tea

커피
coffee

우유
milk

맥주
beer

케이크
cake

빵
bread

아이스크림
ice cream

피자
pizza

사과
apple

수박
watermelon

배
pear

복숭아
peach

귤
mandarine

감
persimmon

바나나
banana

포도
grapes

10 Vegetable

당근
carrot

토마토
tomato

양배추
cabbage

가지
eggplant

마늘
garlic

피망
pepper

파
green onion

오이
cucumber

28

행복하다
happy

슬프다
sad

걱정되다
worried

안심되다
relieved

화나다
angry

초조하다
nervous

두렵다
afraid

놀라다
surprised

12 Building

학교
school

회사
company

도서관
library

공원
park

슈퍼마켓
supermarket

은행
bank

병원
hospital

우체국
post office

13 Transportation

🎧 MP3 W2-13

 자동차
car

 비행기
airplane

 자전거
bicycle

 배
ship

 버스
bus

 트럭
truck

 지하철
subway

 오토바이
motorcycle

 기차
train

14 Hobby

🎧 MP3 W2-14

낚시하다
go fishing

독서하다
read a book

음악 감상하다
listen to music

영화 감상하다
watch a movie

등산하다
go hiking

노래하다
sing a song

체스를 하다
play chess

요리하다
cook

🎧 MP3 W2-15

 축구
soccer

 농구
basketball

 수영
swimming

 조깅
jogging

 테니스
tennis

 배구
volleyball

 골프
golf

 탁구
table tennis

16 Job

회사원
office worker

운전기사
driver

간호사
nurse

운동선수
athlete

가수
singer

교수
professor

화가
painter

경찰
police officer

🎧 MP3 W2-17

바람
wind

비
rain

흐리다
cloudy

맑다
sunny

무지개
rainbow

천둥
thunder

폭풍우
storm

태풍
typhoon

18 Animal

MP3 W2-18

소
cow

쥐
mouse

호랑이
tiger

개
dog

말
horse

토끼
rabbit

원숭이
monkey

뱀
snake

돼지
pig

닭
chicken

19 Daily routine

일어나다
wake up

자다
sleep

세수하다
wash
my face

이를 닦다
brush
my teeth

학교에 가다
go to school

집에 가다
go home

인터넷을 하다
surf
the Internet

운동하다
work out

숙제를 하다
do homework

37

MP3 W2-20

~와
사랑에 빠지다

fall in love
with

~와
데이트하다

go out
with

~와 결혼하다

marry

싸우다

fight

키스하다

kiss

러브레터

love letter

~를 짝사랑하다

have a crush on

나 혼자 끝내는 독학 한국어 첫걸음

독학 한국어

Super Easy Korean for Beginners:
A Self-Study Book

Workbook

넥서스

나 혼자 끝내는 독학 한국어 첫걸음

Workbook

넥서스

✏️ Single Vowels + Diphthongs (1)

Write the following letters on the worksheet.

ㅏ								
ㅐ								
ㅑ								
ㅒ								
ㅓ								
ㅔ								
ㅕ								
ㅖ								
ㅗ								
ㅛ								
ㅜ								
ㅠ								
ㅡ								
ㅣ								

Consonants

Write the following letters on the worksheet.

➔ **book** 19p

ㄱ							
ㄴ							
ㄷ							
ㄹ							
ㅁ							
ㅂ							
ㅅ							
ㅇ							
ㅈ							
ㅊ							
ㅋ							
ㅌ							
ㅍ							
ㅎ							

Combination of consonants and vowels

Write the combination of consonants and vowels down on the worksheet.   ⊕ **book** 20p

	ㅏ	ㅑ	ㅓ	ㅕ	ㅗ	ㅛ	ㅜ	ㅠ	ㅡ	ㅣ
ㄱ										
ㄴ										
ㄷ										
ㄹ										
ㅁ										
ㅂ										
ㅅ										
ㅇ										
ㅈ										
ㅊ										
ㅋ										
ㅌ										
ㅍ										
ㅎ										

 **Diphthongs (2)**

Write the following letters on the worksheet.

➔ **book** 21p

와	왜	외	워	웨	위	의

Double consonants

Write the combination of double consonants and vowels down on the worksheet.

➔ **book** 22p

	ㅏ	ㅓ	ㅗ	ㅜ	ㅡ	ㅣ
ㄲ						
ㄸ						
ㅃ						
ㅆ						
ㅉ						

5

 **Batchim**

Write the combination of consonants and vowels down on the worksheet.

➔ **book** 23p

	아	야	어	여	오	요	우	유	으	이
ㄱ										
ㄴ										
ㄷ										
ㄹ										
ㅁ										
ㅂ										
ㅅ										
ㅇ										
ㅈ										
ㅊ										
ㅋ										
ㅌ										
ㅍ										
ㅎ										

Job

Write the following words on the worksheet.

⊘ **book** 39p

선생님 teacher		
회사원 employee		
학생 student		
운동선수 athlete		
의사 doctor		
기자 reporter		

Country

Write the following words on the worksheet.

⊘ **book** 39p

한국 Korea		
중국 China		
일본 Japan		
베트남 Vietnam		
미국 America		
캐나다 Canada		

Classroom Stuff

Write the following words on the worksheet.

→ book 49p

칠판 blackboard		
의자 chair		
책상 desk		
책 book		
공책 notebook		
볼펜 pen		
필통 pencil case		
연필 pencil		
게시판 bulletin board		
지우개 eraser		
컴퓨터 computer		
노트북 laptop		
시계 clock		

Noun + 이에요/예요

Complete the following words.

→ **book** 36p

ex	
학생 → 학생이에요 | 요리사 → 요리사예요	

요리사 →	
가수 →	
의사 →	
학생 →	
선생님 →	
회사원 →	
의자 →	
시계 →	
컴퓨터 →	
지우개 →	
칠판 →	
책상 →	
볼펜 →	
책 →	

Place

Write the following words on the worksheet.

➔ **book** 56p

학교 school		
교실 classroom		
집 home		
식당 restaurant		
공원 park		
영화관 theater		
카페 café		
공항 airport		
화장실 bathroom		
회사 company		
도서관 library		
병원 hospital		

✎ Direction and Location

Write the following words on the worksheet.

⊙ **book** 59p

위		
아래		
안		
밖		
옆		
앞		
뒤		
오른쪽		
왼쪽		

 **Verb + -아/어요**

Complete the following words.

 book 66p

> **ex**
>
> 놀다 → 놀아요 | 먹다 → 먹어요 | 공부하다 → 공부해요

*가다 →	먹다 →	공부하다 →
*오다 →	읽다 →	운동하다 →
놀다 →	*마시다 →	전화하다 →
받다 →	쉬다 →	말하다 →
*만나다 →	*쓰다 →	쇼핑하다 →

Adjective + -아/어요

Complete the following words.

book 68p

> **ex**
>
> 좋다 → 좋아요 | 싫다 → 싫어요 | 따뜻하다 → 따뜻해요

좋다 →	싫다 →	따뜻하다 →
*비싸다 →	있다 →	시원하다 →
많다 →	적다 →	피곤하다 →
작다 →	*크다 →	친절하다 →
*아프다 →	*덥다 →	조용하다 →

Subject - Object - Verb (Noun + 은/는 + Noun + 을/를 + Verb)

Make sentences using the given words.

⊕ book 67p

ex

> 선생님/집/가다 → 선생님은 집에 가요 |
> 저/커피/마시다 → 저는 커피를 마셔요

*마이클/학교/오다 →	투이/책/읽다 →
동현 씨/편지/쓰다 →	저/밥/먹다 →
양양/친구/만나다 →	*저/집/자다 →

 Verb + -고 싶다

Complete the following words.

⊕ book 76p

ex

> 가다 → 가고 싶어요 | 입다 → 입고 싶어요

오다 →	쉬다 →	공부하다 →
자다 →	배우다 →	운동하다 →
만나다 →	읽다 →	전화하다 →
받다 →	쓰다 →	말하다 →
보다 →	마시다 →	쇼핑하다 →
놀다 →	듣다 →	요리하다 →
저/편지/쓰다 →		*동현 씨/밥/먹다 →

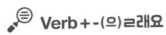

Verb + -(으)ㄹ래요

Complete the following words.

→ book 77p

ex	가다 → 갈래요 ｜ 입다 → 입을래요	

오다 →	받다 →	공부하다 →
마시다 →	먹다 →	운동하다 →
자다 →	읽다 →	전화하다 →
보다 →	*놀다 →	쇼핑하다 →
쓰다 →	*듣다 →	요리하다 →

Verb + -(으)세요

Complete the following words.

→ book 78p

ex	주다 → 주세요 ｜ 입다 → 입으세요	

오다 →	받다 →	공부하다 →
*마시다 →	*먹다 →	운동하다 →
*자다 →	읽다 →	전화하다 →
보다 →	*놀다 →	쇼핑하다 →
쓰다 →	*듣다 →	요리하다 →

*할아버지/안녕히 자다 →	*손님/맛있게 먹다 →
*아빠/커피/마시다 →	투이 씨/책/읽다 →

오다 →	읽다 →	공부하다 →
쓰다 →	먹다 →	운동하다 →

✎ Korean numbers

Write the following words on the worksheet.

→ book 79p

*1 하나		*한 개	
*2 둘		*두 개	
*3 셋		*세 개	
*4 넷		*네 개	
5 다섯		다섯 개	
6 여섯		여섯 개	
7 일곱		일곱 개	
8 여덟[여덜]		여덟 개	
9 아홉		아홉 개	
10 열		열 개	
*20 스물		*스무 개	
30 서른		서른 개	

Verb/Adjective + -았/었어요

Complete the following words.

↪ book 92p

ex

놀다 → 놀았어요 | 재미있다 → 재미있었어요 |
공부하다 → 공부했어요

*가다 →	먹다 →	공부하다 →
*오다 →	읽다 →	운동하다 →
놀다 →	*마시다 →	전화하다 →
받다 →	쉬다 →	말하다 →
*만나다 →	*쓰다 →	쇼핑하다 →
*보다 →	*듣다 →	요리하다 →
좋다 →	싫다 →	따뜻하다 →
*비싸다 →	있다 →	시원하다 →
많다 →	적다 →	피곤하다 →
작다 →	*크다 →	친절하다 →
*아프다 →	*덥다 →	조용하다 →
*나쁘다 →	*힘들다 →	깨끗하다 →

ex

학생 → 학생이었어요 | 요리사 → 요리사였어요

가수 →	선생님 →

 **Time + 에**

Complete the following words.

⊕ **book 93p**

ex	오늘 → 오늘 │ 주말 → 주말에

오늘 →	주말 →
어제 →	낮 →
내일 →	밤 →
그저께 →	아침 →
모레 →	점심 →
지금 →	저녁 →
올해 →	오전 →
매일 →	오후 →
언제 →	–요일 →
*어제/친구/만나다 →	*지금/책/읽다 →

 Time (1) - days and weeks

Write the following words on the worksheet.

⊕ **book 102p**

월요일		
화요일		
수요일		
목요일		
금요일		
토요일		
일요일		

Time (2) - hours & minutes

Write the following words on the worksheet.

⊙ **book** 104p

시		분	
1 (한 시)		1 (일 분)	
2 (두 시)		2 (이 분)	
3 (세 시)		3 (삼 분)	
4 (네 시)		4 (사 분)	
5 (다섯 시)		5 (오 분)	
6 (여섯 시)		6 (육 분)	
7 (일곱 시)		7 (칠 분)	
8 (여덟 시)		8 (팔 분)	
9 (아홉 시)		9 (구 분)	
10 (열 시)		10 (십 분)	
11 (열한 시)		15 (십오 분)	
12 (열두 시)		30 (삼십 분=반)	

가: 몇 시예요?
나: _____ . (9:30)

Date

Write the following words on the worksheet.

 book 105p

월		일	
1 (일 월)		1 (일 일)	
2 (이 월)		2 (이 일)	
3 (삼 월)		3 (삼 일)	
4 (사 월)		4 (사 일)	
5 (오 월)		5 (오 일)	
6 (*유 월)		6 (육 일)	
7 (칠 월)		7 (칠 일)	
8 (팔 월)		8 (팔 일)	
9 (구 월)		9 (구 일)	
10 (*시 월)		10 (십 일)	
11 (십일 월)		16 (십육 일) *[심뉴길]	
12 (십이 월)		30 (삼십 일)	

가: 몇 월 며칠이에요?

나: _____ . (10/16)

안 + Verb/Adjectives

Complete the following words.

→ book 103p

> **ex** 가다 → 안 가다 | 먹다 → 안 먹다 | 일하다 → 일 안 하다

가다 →	먹다 →	공부하다 →
오다 →	읽다 →	운동하다 →
받다 →	쉬다 →	말하다 →
만나다 →	쓰다 →	쇼핑하다 →
보다 →	듣다 →	요리하다 →
좋다 →	싫다 →	*좋아하다 →
비싸다 →	*있다 →	*싫어하다 →
많다 →	적다 →	*피곤하다 →
아프다 →	덥다 →	*조용하다 →
나쁘다 →	힘들다 →	*깨끗하다 →

> **ex** 학생 → 학생이 아니에요 | 요리사 → 요리사가 아니에요

가수 →	선생님 →

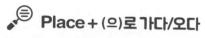

Place + (으)로 가다/오다

Complete the following words.

→ book 103p

ex	앞 → 앞으로 | 뒤 → 뒤로

앞 →	
뒤 →	
위 →	
아래 →	
학교 →	
근처 →	
옆 →	
오른쪽 →	
왼쪽 →	
안 →	
밖 →	
*교실 →	

Verb/Adjective + -지만
Complete the following words.

→ book 112p

ex
> 가다 → 가지만 | 좋다 → 좋지만 | 일하다 → 일하지만

가다 →	먹다 →	공부하다 →
놀다 →	마시다 →	전화하다 →
받다 →	쉬다 →	말하다 →
만나다 →	쓰다 →	쇼핑하다 →
보다 →	듣다 →	요리하다 →
좋다 →	싫다 →	좋아하다 →
비싸다 →	있다 →	싫어하다 →
많다 →	적다 →	피곤하다 →
아프다 →	덥다 →	조용하다 →
나쁘다 →	힘들다 →	깨끗하다 →

ex
> 학생 → 학생이지만 | 요리사 → 요리사지만

가수 →	선생님 →

Verb/Adjective + -았/었지만

Complete the following words.

book 112p

→ book 112p

ex

가다 → 갔지만 | 읽다 → 읽었지만 | 따뜻하다 → 따뜻했지만

*가다 →	먹다 →	공부하다 →
*오다 →	읽다 →	운동하다 →
놀다 →	*마시다 →	전화하다 →
받다 →	쉬다 →	말하다 →
*만나다 →	*쓰다 →	쇼핑하다 →
*보다 →	*듣다 →	요리하다 →
좋다 →	싫다 →	따뜻하다 →
*비싸다 →	있다 →	시원하다 →
많다 →	적다 →	피곤하다 →
작다 →	*크다 →	친절하다 →
*아프다 →	*덥다 →	조용하다 →
*나쁘다 →	힘들다 →	깨끗하다 →

ex

학생 → 학생이었지만 | 요리사 → 요리사였지만

가수 →	선생님 →

(우리) (같이) Verb + -(으)ㄹ까요?

Complete the following words.

→ book 113p

> **ex**
> 가다 → 갈까요? | 먹다 → 먹을까요?

오다 →	받다 →	공부하다 →
마시다 →	먹다 →	운동하다 →
만나다 →	읽다 →	전화하다 →
보다 →	*놀다 →	쇼핑하다 →
쓰다 →	*듣다 →	요리하다 →

 Verb/Adjective + -지 않다

Complete the following words.

→ book 123p

> **ex**
> 가다 → 가지 않다 | 먹다 → 먹지 않다 | 일하다 → 일하지 않다

가다 →	먹다 →	공부하다 →
오다 →	읽다 →	운동하다 →
놀다 →	마시다 →	전화하다 →
받다 →	쉬다 →	말하다 →
만나다 →	쓰다 →	쇼핑하다 →
보다 →	듣다 →	요리하다 →
좋다 →	싫다 →	좋아하다 →

비싸다 →	있다 →	싫어하다 →
많다 →	적다 →	피곤하다 →
작다 →	크다 →	시원하다 →
아프다 →	덥다 →	조용하다 →
나쁘다 →	힘들다 →	깨끗하다 →

Verb/Adjective + -고

Make sentences using the given words.   → book 92p

→ book 92p

> **ex**
> 흐리다/비가 오다 → 흐리고 비가 와요.

이 식당은 맛있다/싸다 →
외국어 공부가 어렵다/재미없다 →
투이는 청소하다/저는 빨래하다 →

Verb/Adjective + -아/어서 (reason)

Make sentences using the given words.   → book 113p

→ book 113p

> **ex**
> 날씨가 맑다/기분이 좋다 → 날씨가 맑아서 기분이 좋아요.

이 식당은 맛있다/좋다 →
청소하다/힘들다 →
*과일이 쌌다/많이 샀다 →

Verb/Adjective + -(으)ㄹ 거예요

Complete the following words.

→ book 124p

ex
가다 → 갈 거예요 ㅣ 재미있다 → 재미있을 거예요

가다 →	먹다 →	공부하다 →
오다 →	읽다 →	운동하다 →
마시다 →	*놀다 →	전화하다 →
보다 →	*듣다 →	요리하다 →
크다 →	싫다 →	따뜻하다 →
예쁘다 →	좋다 →	친절하다 →
아프다 →	*덥다 →	조용하다 →
나쁘다 →	*힘들다 →	깨끗하다 →

ex
학생 → 학생일 거예요 ㅣ 요리사 → 요리사일 거예요

가수 →	선생님 →

Verb/Adjective + -았/었을 거예요

Complete the following words.

→ book 124p

가다 → 갔을 거예요 | 재미있다 → 재미있었을 거예요

*가다 →	먹다 →	공부하다 →
놀다 →	쉬다 →	전화하다 →
받다 →	*쓰다 →	말하다 →
*보다 →	*듣다 →	요리하다 →
*비싸다 →	있다 →	시원하다 →
작다 →	*크다 →	친절하다 →
*아프다 →	*덥다 →	조용하다 →
*나쁘다 →	*힘들다 →	깨끗하다 →

학생 → 학생이었을 거예요 | 요리사 → 요리사였을 거예요

가수 →	선생님 →

Verb/Adjective + -(으)ㄹ까요?

Complete the following words.

⊕ book 124p

가다 → 갈까요? | 먹다 → 먹을까요? | 공부하다 → 공부할까요?

오다 →	읽다 →	운동하다 →
마시다 →	*놀다 →	전화하다 →
보다 →	*듣다 →	요리하다 →
크다 →	*어떻다 →	따뜻하다 →
예쁘다 →	좋다 →	친절하다 →
아프다 →	*덥다 →	조용하다 →
나쁘다 →	*힘들다 →	깨끗하다 →

Verb + -(으)ㄹ 거예요

Complete the following words.

⊕ book 124p

가다 → 갈 거예요 | 먹다 → 먹을 거예요

오다 →	받다 →	공부하다 →
마시다 →	먹다 →	운동하다 →
만나다 →	읽다 →	전화하다 →
보다 →	*놀다 →	쇼핑하다 →
쓰다 →	*듣다 →	요리하다 →

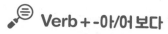 **Verb + -아/어 보다**

Complete the following words.

→ book 133p

> ex
>
> 가다 → 가 보다 | 먹다 → 먹어 보다

*오다 →	쉬다 →	공부하다 →
받다 →	*배우다 →	운동하다 →
*만나다 →	읽다 →	전화하다 →
*보다 → (×)	*마시다 →	쇼핑하다 →
놀다 →	*듣다 →	요리하다 →

Verb + -아/어야 되다

Complete the following words.

→ book 142p

> ex
>
> 가다 → 가야 돼요 | 먹다 → 먹어야 돼요

*오다 →	쉬다 →	공부하다 →
받다 →	*배우다 →	운동하다 →
*만나다 →	읽다 →	전화하다 →
*보다 →	*마시다 →	쇼핑하다 →
놀다 →	*듣다 →	요리하다 →

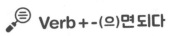 **Verb + -(으)면 되다**

Complete the following words.

→ book 144p

ex	가다 → 가면 돼요 ┃ 먹다 → 먹으면 돼요	

오다 →	받다 →	공부하다 →
마시다 →	먹다 →	운동하다 →
만나다 →	읽다 →	전화하다 →
보다 →	*놀다 →	쇼핑하다 →
쓰다 →	*듣다 →	요리하다 →

 Verb + -아/어도 되다

Complete the following words.

→ book 153p

ex	가다 → 가도 돼요 ┃ 먹다 → 먹어도 돼요	

*오다 →	쉬다 →	공부하다 →
받다 →	*배우다 →	운동하다 →
*만나다 →	읽다 →	전화하다 →
*보다 →	*마시다 →	쇼핑하다 →
놀다 →	*듣다 →	요리하다 →

 **Verb/Adjective + -(으)니까**

Complete the following words.

⊖ **book** 154p

가다 → 가니까 | 좋다 → 좋으니까

가다 →	먹다 →	공부하다 →
오다 →	읽다 →	운동하다 →
마시다 →	*놀다 →	전화하다 →
보다 →	*듣다 →	요리하다 →
크다 →	싫다 →	따뜻하다 →
예쁘다 →	좋다 →	친절하다 →
아프다 →	*덥다 →	조용하다 →
나쁘다 →	*힘들다 →	깨끗하다 →

Casual Speech (Verb/Adjective + -아/어)

Complete the following words.

⊙ book 162p

ex 놀다 → 놀아 | 재미있다 → 재미있어 | 공부하다 → 공부해

*가다 →	먹다 →	공부하다 →
*오다 →	읽다 →	운동하다 →
놀다 →	*마시다 →	전화하다 →
받다 →	쉬다 →	말하다 →
*만나다 →	*쓰다 →	쇼핑하다 →
*보다 →	*듣다 →	요리하다 →
좋다 →	싫다 →	따뜻하다 →
*비싸다 →	있다 →	시원하다 →
많다 →	적다 →	피곤하다 →
작다 →	*크다 →	친절하다 →
*아프다 →	*덥다 →	조용하다 →
*나쁘다 →	힘들다 →	깨끗하다 →

Casual Speech Past (Verb/Adjective + -았/었어, Noun + -이었/였어)

Complete the following words.

→ book 162p

ex

놀다 → 놀았어 | 재미있다 → 재미있었어 | 공부하다 → 공부했어

*가다 →	먹다 →	공부하다 →
*오다 →	읽다 →	운동하다 →
놀다 →	*마시다 →	전화하다 →
받다 →	쉬다 →	말하다 →
*만나다 →	*쓰다 →	쇼핑하다 →
*보다 →	*듣다 →	요리하다 →
좋다 →	싫다 →	따뜻하다 →
*비싸다 →	있다 →	시원하다 →
많다 →	적다 →	피곤하다 →
작다 →	*크다 →	친절하다 →
*아프다 →	*덥다 →	조용하다 →
*나쁘다 →	힘들다 →	깨끗하다 →

ex

학생 → 학생이었어 | 요리사 → 요리사였어

가수 →	선생님 →

33

Casual Speech Future (verb + -(으)ㄹ 거야)

Complete the following words.

book 162p

ex		
가다 → 갈 거야 | 먹다 → 먹을 거야		

가다 →	먹다 →	공부하다 →
오다 →	읽다 →	운동하다 →
마시다 →	*놀다 →	전화하다 →
보다 →	*듣다 →	요리하다 →

 Casual Speech ((Together) Verb + -자)

Complete the following words.

book 163p

ex		
가다 → 가자 | 먹다 → 먹자		

오다 →	받다 →	공부하다 →
마시다 →	먹다 →	운동하다 →
만나다 →	읽다 →	전화하다 →
보다 →	놀다 →	쇼핑하다 →
쓰다 →	듣다 →	요리하다 →

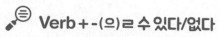

Verb + -(으)ㄹ 수 있다/없다

Complete the following words.

→ book 164p

ex

가다 → 갈 수 있다 | 먹다 → 먹을 수 있다

오다 →	받다 →	공부하다 →
마시다 →	먹다 →	운동하다 →
만나다 →	읽다 →	전화하다 →
보다 →	*놀다 →	쇼핑하다 →
쓰다 →	*듣다 →	요리하다 →

못 + Verb

Complete the following words.

→ book 164p

ex

가다 → 못 가다 | 먹다 → 못 먹다 | 공부하다 → 공부 못 하다

오다 →	받다 →	*공부하다 →
마시다 →	먹다 →	*운동하다 →
만나다 →	읽다 →	*전화하다 →
보다 →	놀다 →	*쇼핑하다 →
쓰다 →	듣다 →	*요리하다 →

나혼자 끝내는 독학 한국어 첫걸음

Answers

Combination of consonants and vowels

	ㅏ	ㅑ	ㅓ	ㅕ	ㅗ	ㅛ	ㅜ	ㅠ	ㅡ	ㅣ
ㄱ	가	갸	거	겨	고	교	구	규	그	기
ㄴ	나	냐	너	녀	노	뇨	누	뉴	느	니
ㄷ	다	댜	더	뎌	도	됴	두	듀	드	디
ㄹ	라	랴	러	려	로	료	루	류	르	리
ㅁ	마	먀	머	며	모	묘	무	뮤	므	미
ㅂ	바	뱌	버	벼	보	뵤	부	뷰	브	비
ㅅ	사	샤	서	셔	소	쇼	수	슈	스	시
ㅇ	아	야	어	여	오	요	우	유	으	이
ㅈ	자	쟈	저	져	조	죠	주	쥬	즈	지
ㅊ	차	챠	처	쳐	초	쵸	추	츄	츠	치
ㅋ	카	캬	커	켜	코	쿄	쿠	큐	크	키
ㅌ	타	탸	터	텨	토	툐	투	튜	트	티
ㅍ	파	퍄	퍼	펴	포	표	푸	퓨	프	피
ㅎ	하	햐	허	혀	호	효	후	휴	흐	히

 **Double consonants**

	ㅏ	ㅓ	ㅗ	ㅜ	ㅡ	ㅣ
ㄲ	까	꺼	꼬	꾸	끄	끼
ㄸ	따	떠	또	뚜	뜨	띠
ㅃ	빠	뻐	뽀	뿌	쁘	삐
ㅆ	싸	써	쏘	쑤	쓰	씨
ㅉ	짜	쩌	쪼	쭈	쯔	찌

 **Batchim**

	아	야	어	여	오	요	우	유	으	이
ㄱ	악	약	억	역	옥	욕	욱	육	윽	익
ㄴ	안	얀	언	연	온	욘	운	윤	은	인
ㄷ	앋	얃	얻	엳	옫	욛	욷	윧	읃	읻
ㄹ	알	얄	얼	열	올	욜	울	율	을	일
ㅁ	암	얌	엄	염	옴	욤	움	윰	음	임
ㅂ	압	얍	업	엽	옵	욥	웁	윱	읍	입
ㅅ	앗	얏	엇	엿	옷	욧	웃	윳	읏	잇
ㅇ	앙	양	엉	영	옹	용	웅	융	응	잉
ㅈ	앚	얒	엊	엿	옺	욪	웆	윶	읒	잊
ㅊ	앛	얓	엋	엋	옻	욫	웇	윷	읓	잋
ㅋ	악	약	억	역	옥	욕	욱	육	윽	익
ㅌ	앝	얕	엍	엹	옽	욭	웉	윹	읕	잍
ㅍ	앞	얖	엎	옆	옾	욮	웊	윺	읖	잎
ㅎ	앟	얗	엏	엫	옿	욯	웋	윻	읗	잏

Noun + 이에요/예요

요리사 → 요리사예요	시계 → 시계예요
가수 → 가수예요	컴퓨터 → 컴퓨터예요
의사 → 의사예요	지우개 → 지우개예요
학생 → 학생이에요	칠판 → 칠판이에요
선생님 → 선생님이에요	책상 → 책상이에요
회사원 → 회사원이에요	볼펜 → 볼펜이에요
의자 → 의자예요	책 → 책이에요

Verb + -아/어요

*가다 → 가요	먹다 → 먹어요	공부하다 → 공부해요
*오다 → 와요	읽다 → 읽어요	운동하다 → 운동해요
놀다 → 놀아요	*마시다 → 마셔요	전화하다 → 전화해요
받다 → 받아요	쉬다 → 쉬어요	말하다 → 말해요
*만나다 → 만나요	*쓰다 → 써요	쇼핑하다 → 쇼핑해요

Adjective + -아/어요

좋다 → 좋아요	싫다 → 싫어요	따뜻하다 → 따뜻해요
*비싸다 → 비싸요	있다 → 있어요	시원하다 → 시원해요
많다 → 많아요	적다 → 적어요	피곤하다 → 피곤해요
작다 → 작아요	*크다 → 커요	친절하다 → 친절해요
*아프다 → 아파요	*덥다 → 더워요	조용하다 → 조용해요

40

💡 Subject - Object - Verb (Noun + 은/는 + Noun + 을/를 + Verb)

*마이클/학교/오다 → 마이클은 학교에 와요	투이/책/읽다 → 투이는 책을 읽어요
동현 씨/편지/쓰다 → 동현 씨는 편지를 써요	저/밥/먹다 → 저는 밥을 먹어요
양양/친구/만나다 → 양양은 친구를 만나요	*저/집/자다 → 저는 집에서 자요

💡 Verb + -고 싶다

오다 → 오고 싶어요	쉬다 → 쉬고 싶어요	공부하다 → 공부하고 싶어요
자다 → 자고 싶어요	배우다 → 배우고 싶어요	운동하다 → 운동하고 싶어요
만나다 → 만나고 싶어요	읽다 → 읽고 싶어요	전화하다 → 전화하고 싶어요
받다 → 받고 싶어요	쓰다 → 쓰고 싶어요	말하다 → 말하고 싶어요
보다 → 보고 싶어요	마시다 → 마시고 싶어요	쇼핑하다 → 쇼핑하고 싶어요
놀다 → 놀고 싶어요	듣다 → 듣고 싶어요	요리하다 → 요리하고 싶어요

저/편지/쓰다 → 저는 편지를 쓰고 싶어요.	*동현 씨/밥/먹다 → 동현 씨는 밥을 먹고 싶어 해요.

💡 Verb + -(으)ㄹ래요

오다 → 올래요	받다 → 받을래요	공부하다 → 공부할래요
마시다 → 마실래요	먹다 → 먹을래요	운동하다 → 운동할래요
자다 → 잘래요	읽다 → 읽을래요	전화하다 → 전화할래요
보다 → 볼래요	*놀다 → 놀래요	쇼핑하다 → 쇼핑할래요
쓰다 → 쓸래요	*듣다 → 들을래요	요리하다 → 요리할래요

💡 Verb + -(으)세요

오다 → 오세요	받다 → 받으세요	공부하다 → 공부하세요
*마시다 → 드세요	*먹다 → 드세요	운동하다 → 운동하세요
*자다 → 주무세요	읽다 → 읽으세요	전화하다 → 전화하세요
보다 → 보세요	*놀다 → 노세요	쇼핑하다 → 쇼핑하세요
쓰다 → 쓰세요	*듣다 → 들으세요	요리하다 → 요리하세요

*할아버지/안녕히 자다 → 할아버지, 안녕히 주무세요	*손님/맛있게 먹다 → 손님, 맛있게 드세요
*아빠/커피/마시다 → 아빠, 커피 드세요	투이 씨/책/읽다 → 투이 씨, 책을 읽으세요

오다 → 오지 마세요	읽다 → 읽지 마세요	공부하다 → 공부하지 마세요
쓰다 → 쓰지 마세요	먹다 → 먹지 마세요	운동하다 → 운동하지 마세요

💡 Verb/Adjective + -았/었어요

*가다 → 갔어요	먹다 → 먹었어요	공부하다 → 공부했어요
*오다 → 왔어요	읽다 → 읽었어요	운동하다 → 운동했어요
놀다 → 놀았어요	*마시다 → 마셨어요	전화하다 → 전화했어요
받다 → 받았어요	쉬다 → 쉬었어요	말하다 → 말했어요
*만나다 → 만났어요	*쓰다 → 썼어요	쇼핑하다 → 쇼핑했어요
*보다 → 봤어요	*듣다 → 들었어요	요리하다 → 요리했어요
좋다 → 좋았어요	싫다 → 싫었어요	따뜻하다 → 따뜻했어요

*비싸다 → 비쌌어요	있다 → 있었어요	시원하다 → 시원했어요
많다 → 많았어요	적다 → 적었어요	피곤하다 → 피곤했어요
작다 → 작았어요	*크다 → 컸어요	친절하다 → 친절했어요
*아프다 → 아팠어요	*덥다 → 더웠어요	조용하다 → 조용했어요
*나쁘다 → 나빴어요	*힘들다 → 힘들었어요	깨끗하다 → 깨끗했어요

가수 → 가수였어요	선생님 → 선생님이었어요

💡 Time + 에

오늘 → 오늘	주말 → 주말에
어제 → 어제	낮 → 낮에
내일 → 내일	밤 → 밤에
그저께 → 그저께	아침 → 아침에
모레 → 모레	점심 → 점심에
지금 → 지금	저녁 → 저녁에
올해 → 올해	오전 → 오전에
매일 → 매일	오후 → 오후에
언제 → 언제	–요일 → –요일에
*어제/친구/만나다 → 어제 친구를 만났어요	*지금/책/읽다 → 지금 책을 읽어요

가: 몇 시예요?
나: 아홉 시 삼십 분이에요./아홉 시 반이에요. (9:30)

 Date

가: 몇 월 며칠이에요?
나: 시 월 십육 일이에요. (10/16)

안 + Verb/Adjectives

가다 → 안 가다	먹다 → 안 먹다	공부하다 → 공부 안 하다
오다 → 안 오다	읽다 → 안 읽다	운동하다 → 운동 안 하다
받다 → 안 받다	쉬다 → 안 쉬다	말하다 → 말 안 하다
만나다 → 안 만나다	쓰다 → 안 쓰다	쇼핑하다 → 쇼핑 안 하다
보다 → 안 보다	듣다 → 안 듣다	요리하다 → 요리 안 하다
좋다 → 안 좋다	싫다 → 안 싫다	*좋아하다 → 안 좋아하다
비싸다 → 안 비싸다	*있다 → 없다	*싫어하다 → 안 싫어하다
많다 → 안 많다	적다 → 안 적다	*피곤하다 → 안 피곤하다
아프다 → 안 아프다	덥다 → 안 덥다	*조용하다 → 안 조용하다
나쁘다 → 안 나쁘다	힘들다 → 안 힘들다	*깨끗하다 → 안 깨끗하다

가수 → 가수가 아니에요	선생님 → 선생님이 아니에요

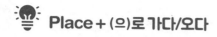 **Place + (으)로 가다/오다**

앞 → 앞으로	옆 → 옆으로
뒤 → 뒤로	오른쪽 → 오른쪽으로
위 → 위로	왼쪽 → 왼쪽으로
아래 → 아래로	안 → 안으로
학교 → 학교로	밖 → 밖으로
근처 → 근처로	*교실 → 교실로

 Verb/Adjective + -지만

가다 → 가지만	먹다 → 먹지만	공부하다 → 공부하지만
놀다 → 놀지만	마시다 → 마시지만	전화하다 → 전화하지만
받다 → 받지만	쉬다 → 쉬지만	말하다 → 말하지만
만나다 → 만나지만	쓰다 → 쓰지만	쇼핑하다 → 쇼핑하지만
보다 → 보지만	듣다 → 듣지만	요리하다 → 요리하지만
좋다 → 좋지만	싫다 → 싫지만	좋아하다 → 좋아하지만
비싸다 → 비싸지만	있다 → 있지만	싫어하다 → 싫어하지만
많다 → 많지만	적다 → 적지만	피곤하다 → 피곤하지만
아프다 → 아프지만	덥다 → 덥지만	조용하다 → 조용하지만
나쁘다 → 나쁘지만	힘들다 → 힘들지만	깨끗하다 → 깨끗하지만

가수 → 가수지만	선생님 → 선생님이지만

Verb/Adjective + -았/었지만

*가다 → 갔지만	먹다 → 먹었지만	공부하다 → 공부했지만
*오다 → 왔지만	읽다 → 읽었지만	운동하다 → 운동했지만
놀다 → 놀았지만	*마시다 → 마셨지만	전화하다 → 전화했지만
받다 → 받았지만	쉬다 → 쉬었지만	말하다 → 말했지만
*만나다 → 만났지만	*쓰다 → 썼지만	쇼핑하다 → 쇼핑했지만
*보다 → 봤지만	*듣다 → 들었지만	요리하다 → 요리했지만
좋다 → 좋았지만	싫다 → 싫었지만	따뜻하다 → 따뜻했지만
*비싸다 → 비쌌지만	있다 → 있었지만	시원하다 → 시원했지만
많다 → 많았지만	적다 → 적었지만	피곤하다 → 피곤했지만
작다 → 작았지만	*크다 → 컸지만	친절하다 → 친절했지만
*아프다 → 아팠지만	*덥다 → 더웠지만	조용하다 → 조용했지만
*나쁘다 → 나빴지만	힘들다 → 힘들었지만	깨끗하다 → 깨끗했지만

가수 → 가수였지만	선생님 → 선생님이었지만

 (우리) (같이) Verb + -(으)ㄹ까요?

오다 → 올까요?	받다 → 받을까요?	공부하다 → 공부할까요?
마시다 → 마실까요?	먹다 → 먹을까요?	운동하다 → 운동할까요?
만나다 → 만날까요?	읽다 → 읽을까요?	전화하다 → 전화할까요?
보다 → 볼까요?	*놀다 → 놀까요?	쇼핑하다 → 쇼핑할까요?
쓰다 → 쓸까요?	*듣다 → 들을까요?	요리하다 → 요리할까요?

46

Verb/Adjective + -지 않다

가다 → 가지 않다	먹다 → 먹지 않다	공부하다 → 공부하지 않다
오다 → 오지 않다	읽다 → 읽지 않다	운동하다 → 운동하지 않다
놀다 → 놀지 않다	마시다 → 마시지 않다	전화하다 → 전화하지 않다
받다 → 받지 않다	쉬다 → 쉬지 않다	말하다 → 말하지 않다
만나다 → 만나지 않다	쓰다 → 쓰지 않다	쇼핑하다 → 쇼핑하지 않다
보다 → 보지 않다	듣다 → 듣지 않다	요리하다 → 요리하지 않다
좋다 → 좋지 않다	싫다 → 싫지 않다	좋아하다 → 좋아하지 않다
비싸다 → 비싸지 않다	있다 → 있지 않다	싫어하다 → 싫어하지 않다
많다 → 많지 않다	적다 → 적지 않다	피곤하다 → 피곤하지 않다
작다 → 작지 않다	크다 → 크지 않다	시원하다 → 시원하지 않다
아프다 → 아프지 않다	덥다 → 덥지 않다	조용하다 → 조용하지 않다
나쁘다 → 나쁘지 않다	힘들다 → 힘들지 않다	깨끗하다 → 깨끗하지 않다

Verb/Adjective + -고

이 식당은 맛있다/싸다 → 이 식당은 맛있고 싸요.
외국어 공부가 어렵다/재미없다 → 외국어 공부가 어렵고 재미없어요.
투이는 청소하다/저는 빨래하다 → 투이는 청소하고 저는 빨래해요.

Verb/Adjective + -아/어서 (reason)

이 식당은 맛있다/좋다 → 이 식당은 맛있어서 좋아요.
청소하다/힘들다 → 청소해서 힘들어요.
*과일이 쌌다/많이 샀다 → 과일이 싸서 많이 샀어요.

 Verb/Adjective + -(으)ㄹ 거예요

가다 → 갈 거예요	먹다 → 먹을 거예요	공부하다 → 공부할 거예요
오다 → 올 거예요	읽다 → 읽을 거예요	운동하다 → 운동할 거예요
마시다 → 마실 거예요	*놀다 → 놀 거예요	전화하다 → 전화할 거예요
보다 → 볼 거예요	*듣다 → 들을 거예요	요리하다 → 요리할 거예요
크다 → 클 거예요	싫다 → 싫을 거예요	따뜻하다 → 따뜻할 거예요
예쁘다 → 예쁠 거예요	좋다 → 좋을 거예요	친절하다 → 친절할 거예요
아프다 → 아플 거예요	*덥다 → 더울 거예요	조용하다 → 조용할 거예요
나쁘다 → 나쁠 거예요	*힘들다 → 힘들 거예요	깨끗하다 → 깨끗할 거예요

가수 → 가수일 거예요	선생님 → 선생님일 거예요

Verb/Adjective + -았/었을 거예요

*가다 → 갔을 거예요	먹다 → 먹었을 거예요	공부하다 → 공부했을 거예요
놀다 → 놀았을 거예요	쉬다 → 쉬었을 거예요	전화하다 → 전화했을 거예요
받다 → 받았을 거예요	*쓰다 → 썼을 거예요	말하다 → 말했을 거예요
*보다 → 봤을 거예요	*듣다 → 들었을 거예요	요리하다 → 요리했을 거예요
*비싸다 → 비쌌을 거예요	있다 → 있었을 거예요	시원하다 → 시원했을 거예요
작다 → 작았을 거예요	*크다 → 컸을 거예요	친절하다 → 친절했을 거예요
*아프다 → 아팠을 거예요	*덥다 → 더웠을 거예요	조용하다 → 조용했을 거예요
*나쁘다 → 나빴을 거예요	*힘들다 → 힘들었을 거예요	깨끗하다 → 깨끗했을 거예요

가수 → 가수였을 거예요	선생님 → 선생님이었을 거예요

Verb/Adjective + -(으)ㄹ까요?

오다 → 올까요?	읽다 → 읽을까요?	운동하다 → 운동할까요?
마시다 → 마실까요?	*놀다 → 놀까요?	전화하다 → 전화할까요?
보다 → 볼까요?	*듣다 → 들을까요?	요리하다 → 요리할까요?
크다 → 클까요?	*어떻다 → 어떨까요?	따뜻하다 → 따뜻할까요?
예쁘다 → 예쁠까요?	좋다 → 좋을까요?	친절하다 → 친절할까요?
아프다 → 아플까요?	*덥다 → 더울까요?	조용하다 → 조용할까요?
나쁘다 → 나쁠까요?	*힘들다 → 힘들까요?	깨끗하다 → 깨끗할까요?

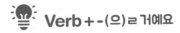 **Verb + -(으)ㄹ 거예요**

오다 → 올 거예요	받다 → 받을 거예요	공부하다 → 공부할 거예요
마시다 → 마실 거예요	먹다 → 먹을 거예요	운동하다 → 운동할 거예요
만나다 → 만날 거예요	읽다 → 읽을 거예요	전화하다 → 전화할 거예요
보다 → 볼 거예요	*놀다 → 놀 거예요	쇼핑하다 → 쇼핑할 거예요
쓰다 → 쓸 거예요	*듣다 → 들을 거예요	요리하다 → 요리할 거예요

Verb + -아/어 보다

*오다 → 와 보다	쉬다 → 쉬어 보다	공부하다 → 공부해 보다
받다 → 받아 보다	*배우다 → 배워 보다	운동하다 → 운동해 보다
*만나다 → 만나 보다	읽다 → 읽어 보다	전화하다 → 전화해 보다
*보다 → (×)	*마시다 → 마셔 보다	쇼핑하다 → 쇼핑해 보다
놀다 → 놀아 보다	*듣다 → 들어 보다	요리하다 → 요리해 보다

Verb + -아/어야 되다

*오다 → 와야 돼요	쉬다 → 쉬어야 돼요	공부하다 → 공부해야 돼요
받다 → 받아야 돼요	*배우다 → 배워야 돼요	운동하다 → 운동해야 돼요
*만나다 → 만나야 돼요	읽다 → 읽어야 돼요	전화하다 → 전화해야 돼요
*보다 → 봐야 돼요	*마시다 → 마셔야 돼요	쇼핑하다 → 쇼핑해야 돼요
놀다 → 놀아야 돼요	*듣다 → 들어야 돼요	요리하다 → 요리해야 돼요

 **Verb + -(으)면 되다**

오다 → 오면 돼요	받다 → 받으면 돼요	공부하다 → 공부하면 돼요
마시다 → 마시면 돼요	먹다 → 먹으면 돼요	운동하다 → 운동하면 돼요
만나다 → 만나면 돼요	읽다 → 읽으면 돼요	전화하다 → 전화하면 돼요
보다 → 보면 돼요	*놀다 → 놀면 돼요	쇼핑하다 → 쇼핑하면 돼요
쓰다 → 쓰면 돼요	*듣다 → 들으면 돼요	요리하다 → 요리하면 돼요

Verb + -아/어도 되다

*오다 → 와도 돼요	쉬다 → 쉬어도 돼요	공부하다 → 공부해도 돼요
받다 → 받아도 돼요	*배우다 → 배워도 돼요	운동하다 → 운동해도 돼요
*만나다 → 만나도 돼요	읽다 → 읽어도 돼요	전화하다 → 전화해도 돼요
*보다 → 봐도 돼요	*마시다 → 마셔도 돼요	쇼핑하다 → 쇼핑해도 돼요
놀다 → 놀아도 돼요	*듣다 → 들어도 돼요	요리하다 → 요리해도 돼요

Verb/Adjective + -(으)니까

가다 → 가니까	먹다 → 먹으니까	공부하다 → 공부하니까
오다 → 오니까	읽다 → 읽으니까	운동하다 → 운동하니까
마시다 → 마시니까	*놀다 → 노니까	전화하다 → 전화하니까
보다 → 보니까	*듣다 → 들으니까	요리하다 → 요리하니까

크다 → 크니까	싫다 → 싫으니까	따뜻하다 → 따뜻하니까
예쁘다 → 예쁘니까	좋다 → 좋으니까	친절하다 → 친절하니까
아프다 → 아프니까	*덥다 → 더우니까	조용하다 → 조용하니까
나쁘다 → 나쁘니까	*힘들다 → 힘드니까	깨끗하다 → 깨끗하니까

💡 Casual Speech (Verb/Adjective + -아/어)

*가다 → 가	먹다 → 먹어	공부하다 → 공부해
*오다 → 와	읽다 → 읽어	운동하다 → 운동해
놀다 → 놀아	*마시다 → 마셔	전화하다 → 전화해
받다 → 받아	쉬다 → 쉬어	말하다 → 말해
*만나다 → 만나	*쓰다 → 써	쇼핑하다 → 쇼핑해
*보다 → 봐	*듣다 → 들어	요리하다 → 요리해
좋다 → 좋아	싫다 → 싫어	따뜻하다 → 따뜻해
*비싸다 → 비싸	있다 → 있어	시원하다 → 시원해
많다 → 많아	적다 → 적어	피곤하다 → 피곤해
작다 → 작아	*크다 → 커	친절하다 → 친절해
*아프다 → 아파	*덥다 → 더워	조용하다 → 조용해
*나쁘다 → 나빠	힘들다 →힘들어	깨끗하다 → 깨끗해

Casual Speech Past (Verb/Adjective + -았/었어, Noun + -이었/였어)

*가다 → 갔어	먹다 → 먹었어	공부하다 → 공부했어
*오다 → 왔어	읽다 → 읽었어	운동하다 → 운동했어
놀다 → 놀았어	*마시다 → 마셨어	전화하다 → 전화했어
받다 → 받았어	쉬다 → 쉬었어	말하다 → 말했어
*만나다 → 만났어	*쓰다 → 썼어	쇼핑하다 → 쇼핑했어
*보다 → 봤어	*듣다 → 들었어	요리하다 → 요리했어
좋다 → 좋았어	싫다 → 싫었어	따뜻하다 → 따뜻했어
*비싸다 → 비쌌어	있다 → 있었어	시원하다 → 샤워했어
많다 → 많았어	적다 → 적었어	피곤하다 → 피곤했어
작다 → 작았어	*크다 → 컸어	친절하다 → 친절했어
*아프다 → 아팠어	*덥다 → 더웠어	조용하다 → 조용했어
*나쁘다 → 나빴어	힘들다 → 힘들었어	깨끗하다 → 깨끗했어

가수 → 가수였어	선생님 → 선생님이었어

Casual Speech Future (verb + -(으)ㄹ 거야)

가다 → 갈 거야	먹다 → 먹을 거야	공부하다 → 공부할 거야
오다 → 올 거야	읽다 → 읽을 거야	운동하다 → 운동할 거야
마시다 → 마실 거야	*놀다 → 놀 거야	전화하다 → 전화할 거야
보다 → 볼 거야	*듣다 → 들을 거야	요리하다 → 요리할 거야

 Casual Speech ((Together) Verb + -자)

오다 → 오자	받다 → 받자	공부하다 → 공부하자
마시다 → 마시자	먹다 → 먹자	운동하다 → 운동하자
만나다 → 만나자	읽다 → 읽자	전화하다 → 전화하자
보다 → 보자	놀다 → 놀자	쇼핑하다 → 쇼핑하자
쓰다 → 쓰자	듣다 → 듣자	요리하다 → 요리하자

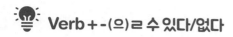 **Verb + -(으)ㄹ 수 있다/없다**

오다 → 올 수 있다	받다 → 받을 수 있다	공부하다 → 공부할 수 있다
마시다 → 마실 수 있다	먹다 → 먹을 수 있다	운동하다 → 운동할 수 있다
만나다 → 만날 수 있다	읽다 → 읽을 수 있다	전화하다 → 전화할 수 있다
보다 → 볼 수 있다	*놀다 → 놀 수 있다	쇼핑하다 → 쇼핑할 수 있다
쓰다 → 쓸 수 있다	*듣다 → 들을 수 있다	요리하다 → 요리할 수 있다

못 + Verb

오다 → 못 오다	받다 → 못 받다	*공부하다 → 공부 못 하다
마시다 → 못 마시다	먹다 → 못 먹다	*운동하다 → 운동 못 하다
만나다 → 못 만나다	읽다 → 못 읽다	*전화하다 → 전화 못 하다
보다 → 못 보다	놀다 → 못 놀다	*쇼핑하다 → 쇼핑 못 하다
쓰다 → 못 쓰다	듣다 → 못 듣다	*요리하다 → 요리 못 하다